White Ma
Book for E

DISCLAIMER

All content in this book is presented for informational and inspirational purposes only. It draws upon historical traditions, folklore, and modern magical practices, but presents them in an original voice. The content is not intended as a substitute for medical, psychological, legal, or professional advice.

While this book discusses themes found in Wicca, Hermeticism, folk magic, and other esoteric systems, it is not affiliated with any official organization, church, or tradition. The author does not claim lineage, authority, or certification in any religious or magical order. All references to historical figures, deities, or cultural practices are made with respect, and no infringement is intended.

The spells, rituals, and terms described in this book are original creations of the author. Any resemblance to existing works, characters, or branded names is purely coincidental. The terms "Wicca," "Hermeticism," and other named systems are used descriptively and do not imply endorsement or ownership.

By reading or applying the practices described in this book, you agree that you are solely responsible for your actions, choices, and any outcomes that result. No warranty is made regarding the outcome of any practice described herein. The author and publisher accept no liability for how this material is interpreted or used.

All rights reserved © 2025

Contents

INTRODUCTION: AWAKENING TO THE LIGHT OF MAGIC 7
    THE ESSENCE OF WHITE MAGIC 7
    ECHOES OF LIGHT THROUGH HISTORY 8
    A LIVING TRADITION 10
    WICCAN NATURE-MYSTICISM 11
    HERMETIC MICROCOSM ↔ MACROCOSM 13
    FOLK MAGIC OF HEARTH & HEDGE 15

ILLUMINATING THE PATH – PRINCIPLES AND ETHICS 19
    CIRCLE OF VIRTUOUS ACCORD (RITUAL) 20
    CONSECRATION OF SINCERE PURPOSE (SPELL) 25
    VOW OF THE RADIANT PATH (RITUAL) 27
    QUADRIVIUM OF SACRED WINDS (SPELL) 30
    FORTUNE'S BENEFIC PURSE (CHARM) 33

SACRED SPACES & TOOLS OF THE CRAFT 36
    SANCTUM ANOINTMENT RITE (RITUAL) 37
    INSTRUMENTS OF SACRED PURPOSE (RITUAL) 40
    HEARTH-WARD CLEANSING (SPELL) 43
    GUARDIAN OF THE THRESHOLD (CHARM) 46

SPELLS OF PROTECTION AND PURIFICATION 48

AEGIS OF THE ELEMENTAL QUADRANT (SPELL) 49

SPECULUM SANCTUS DEFLECTORIUM (CHARM) 52

LUSTRATION OF SALT AND GREEN (RITUAL) 54

REFLECTIVE AEGIS OF SILVER (SPELL) 56

ELEMENTAL ALLIES – EARTH, AIR, FIRE, WATER, SPIRIT 59

VESSEL OF VERDANT PROSPERITY (EARTH RITUAL) 62

WINDS OF INNER KNOWING (AIR SPELL) 64

THE HOLLOW FIRE ASCENSION (FIRE RITUAL) 65

SELENIC TIDE PURIFICATION (WATER SPELL) 67

ETHEREAL CONFLUENCE BENEDICTION (SPIRIT RITUAL) 69

MOONLIGHT AND SUNFIRE – LUNAR & SOLAR MAGIC 72

DARKMOON GENESIS SPELL (NEW MOON) 75

LUNAR APEX CONVERGENCE (FULL MOON RITUAL) 77

TIDE OF THE SILVER CRESCENT (WAXING MOON SPELL) 79

DIMINISHING SHADOWS INCANTATION (WANING MOON SPELL) 80

HELIOS GATE CONSECRATION (RITUAL) 82

GOLDEN RAY TALISMAN (CHARM) 84

WEAVING SPELLS – CRAFTING WITH INTENT AND SYMBOL 86

SPHERE OF ILLUMINATED WILL (RITUAL) 87

GLYPH OF FOCUSED MANIFESTATION (SIGIL SPELL) 89

EMPYREAL SIGIL OF FORTITUDE (CHARM) 91

SCRIPT OF ARCANE EMANATION (SPELL - MANIFESTATION THROUGH WRITING) 92

HEALING LIGHT – SPELLS FOR WELLNESS & RENEWAL 95

LUMINAL BALM CANDLE (SPELL) 96

WATERS OF REJUVENATION RITE (RITUAL) 98

VITALITY SACHET OF THE GREEN GRACES (CHARM) 100

GEM OF RESTORATIVE RADIANCE (SPELL) 101

CIRCLE OF PROTECTION – WARDING & BANISHING .. 104

AEGIS TALISMAN ARTIFICE (SPELL) 105

EXILE OF THE CROSSWIND VORTEX (RITUAL) 108

WARDENS' VESSEL OF DOMESTIC AEGIS (WITCH BOTTLE PROTECTION SPELL) 111

REDOUBT OF IRON AND BRINE (MINIMALIST PROTECTION CHARM) 114

HEART OF THE WITCH – LOVE, FRIENDSHIP & HARMONY 116

MYSTERIA ROSARUM – LUX CORDIS INCANTATIO (SPELL) 117

CANDLE OF CONVERGING PATHS (SPELL) 119

CONCORDIA HOUSEHOLD INVOCATION (RITUAL) 121

THREAD OF AMITY BOND (CHARM - KNOT MAGIC FOR MUTUAL SUPPORT AND FRIENDSHIP) 124

PROSPERITY & PLENTY – ABUNDANCE MAGIC 126

EMERALD FLAME OF ABUNDANCE (WEALTH & OPPORTUNITY CANDLE SPELL) 127

AURIC CANDLE OF HONEY-SPICED PROSPERITY (CANDLE SPELL FOR SWEET, STEADY ABUNDANCE)... 129

GNOME GUARDIAN'S OFFERING (EARTH SPIRIT INVITATION & HOME PROSPERITY SPELL)...131

ARCANE COFFER OF PERPETUAL BLESSINGS (PROSPERITY SPELL BOX FOR ONGOING ABUNDANCE) 133

CORNUCOPIA POUCH OF FORTUNE (PROSPERITY CHARM FOR ONGOING ABUNDANCE) 135

RITE OF AUTUMNAL THANKSGIVING (RITUAL)...............................137

EMBLEM OF ASCENDANT VOCATION (CAREER ADVANCEMENT & PROJECT SUCCESS SPELL) 139

Introduction: Awakening to the Light of Magic

A single candle flame dances in the twilight, casting gentle shadows that spark an ancient remembrance within the soul. In this hush of expectation, you stand at the threshold of an **extraordinary journey**: White Magic, a path that merges timeless wisdom with your own heartfelt aspirations. This book will guide you in **channeling the elements, lunar and solar currents**, and the **power of the divine Spirit** toward healing, protection, and growth.

Yet, as you read these words, you also walk in the footprints of countless seekers—wise folk, healers, and mystics—who **kindled** their lamps in ages past. Indeed, the flame illuminating your path has danced in many forms before: flickering torches in Egyptian temples, hearth fires in Celtic groves, and the humble rushlights of medieval kitchens where cunning folk whispered protective charms. In every epoch, practitioners of White Magic have stood at the **threshold of the invisible**, striving to bring forth goodness, solace, and renewal.

The Essence of White Magic

White Magic is rooted in **compassion, reverence for life**, and a **commitment to do no harm**. As you explore spells and rituals, you learn to shape **subtle energies** without violating the natural flow of life. Whether through calling on the elements or reciting extended prayers under the moon, White Magic weaves your will into **harmony with the**

Universal Light—that divine source that breathes through every living thing.

In many ancient teachings—such as the **mystery cults** of classical Greece or the **wisdom schools** of Alexandria—there was a shared notion of a luminous force that unites all creation. Philosophers and priestesses alike spoke of this cosmic radiance as **the living essence** that stirs within each soul. Practitioners of what we now call "white" or benevolent magic sought to channel that essence for the well-being of the community: to **heal the sick**, **bless the harvest**, and **ward off harm**. In this continuum, White Magic stands as the art of **aligning** with that higher vibrational field, ensuring our works reflect **love** rather than **domination**.

Today, we continue that lineage, viewing White Magic not as superstition but as a **soulful technology**—a means of dialoguing with forces both seen and unseen. You will discover that each spell or charm is more than a formula: it is a song of communion with the wild, breathing heart of nature. Far from being locked in antiquity, White Magic evolves with every generation, morphing into new shapes that accommodate fresh cultural insights while preserving its **ethical core**.

Echoes of Light Through History

Historic glimpses reveal how the roots of benevolent magic run **deep and diverse**:

- **Ancient Egypt**: Temple healers practiced ritual purification, using incantations to align the ka (spiritual essence) with the gods' favor. Papyrus scrolls recount how white-robed priests invoked the nurturing power of deities

like Isis, seeking to cure ailments and shield the living from malevolent forces.
- **Greek and Hellenistic Worlds**: Philosophers and mystics in the Orphic and Eleusinian mysteries believed in the soul's purification through sacred rites. They used **incense, hymns, and symbolic gestures** to evoke the cosmic harmony of the **Heavens**—a precursor to the principle "as above, so below" that you will explore in Hermetic teachings.
- **Celtic and Druidic Traditions**: In forest groves, druids performed blessings for abundant harvests and communal well-being. They believed in the interplay of Earth, sky, and the **Otherworld**, weaving their ceremonies with oak leaves, sacred fires, and whispered verses that honored life's cyclical nature. Here, the seeds of Western folk magic found fertile ground, eventually sprouting into local customs of herbal healing and protective charms.
- **Medieval Europe and Cunning Folk**: Throughout the Middle Ages, local "wise ones" or "cunning folk" served their communities by crafting healing poultices, diagnosing spiritual afflictions, and reciting blessings. Although often wary of ecclesiastical suspicion, these practitioners upheld a tradition of **white** or **benign** magic, emphasizing the sanctity of life and the power of prayerful intention. Their legacy persists in the modern emphasis on healing, home protection, and respectful co-existence with nature's energies.
- **Renaissance and Hermetic Revival**: With the rediscovery of classical texts in Europe, scholars merged Platonic, Hermetic, and Christian ideals. Figures like Marsilio Ficino and other Renaissance magi believed that by **studying the stars**, aligning with planetary influences, and venerating the Divine, one could elevate the spirit to a state of *"angelic harmony."* This epoch laid key

foundations for the Western esoteric traditions that continue to shape White Magic's philosophical and mystical framework.

The thread binding these eras is the **conviction** that magic—when practiced ethically—can act as a **bridge** between mortal endeavor and cosmic grandeur. From temple altars to quiet hearths, from hidden forest circles to modern living rooms, White Magic's protective and healing essence has shone across centuries, a **steady glow** amid ever-shifting cultural tides.

A Living Tradition

This book reflects an **integrated approach**, weaving insights from multiple esoteric lineages into a coherent practice for the **modern seeker**:

- **Wicca's** love of nature and **ethical focus on Harm None** calls us to cherish the Earth as both mother and teacher. This emphasis on **reverence** and **responsibility** underpins every spell in the pages ahead, ensuring that personal power flourishes within an **awareness of the greater good**.
- **Hermetic principles** reveal the microcosm and macrocosm as **mirrors**: what occurs within our inner worlds resonates in the cosmos at large, and vice versa. You will find references to cosmic correspondences, elemental harmonies, and the notion that **transformation of the self** is key to transforming one's reality.
- **Folk magic** offers **simplicity** and **practicality**, handed down through countless generations of **wise folk** who used everyday items—common herbs, household objects, seasonal rituals—to weave blessings and keep negativity

at bay. Folk spells remind us that magic thrives in the **ordinary** as much as in the exalted.

In uniting these streams, you will discover a tradition that is nurturing yet transformative, ancient yet adaptable to our modern world. Each tradition has its own *language* of symbols and rites, but all converge on the same luminous principle: that human will, aligned with love and respect, can uplift our experiences and help guide the quiet unfolding of our lives with grace and purpose.

Wiccan Nature-Mysticism

"**Harm None**—and honour the living Earth"

Core Idea

Wicca treats the planet as a sentient, sacred body. When you bless a seed, recycle a bottle, or whisper thanks to the full Moon, you're not *adding* spirituality to nature—you're *recognising* the divinity already there.

The pentacle is one of the most powerful and central symbols in Wicca. It is a five-pointed star enclosed within a circle, representing the harmony of the five sacred elements—Earth, Air, Fire, Water, and Spirit. More than a symbol, the pentacle is a map of Wicca's deepest belief: that the Earth is alive, sacred, and interconnected. When a Wiccan traces the pentacle, they are not drawing lines in the air—they are calling upon the forces of nature, recognising that every stone, flame, breath, and tear is part of a greater whole. The pentacle is a reminder that the magic of the world flows through all things, and that to honor the elements is to honor the sacred life of the planet itself.

Beginner Daily Practice (10 minutes)

1. **Ground & Centre (1 min)** – Stand barefoot, inhale through nose, imagine roots growing into soil.
2. **Sky-Reach (1 min)** – Stretch arms upward, exhale slowly, picture starlight pouring down.
3. **Gratitude Whisper (30 sec)** – "Earth-Mother, thank you for ____." (name one gift—food, shade tree, rainfall).
4. **Mini-Offering (1 min)** – Pour a spoon of clean water at a plant's base or scatter a few bird seeds.
5. **Journal (6 min)** – Record today's weather, moon phase, and one personal emotion. Over weeks you'll *see* how inner tides echo outer ones.

Common Pitfalls & Safeguards

- **Eco-Guilt Spiral** – Perfection isn't required. Aim for *progress*: swap plastic wrap for beeswax, volunteer once a month.
- **Cultural Mix-&-Match** – It's fine to explore, but study sources respectfully; don't lift closed-practice rites.
- **Spell-First Thinking** – Ethics come *before* technique. Ask: "Does this help life thrive?" If uncertain, revise or refrain.

Hermetic Microcosm ↔ Macrocosm

"As above, so below; as within, so without"

Core Idea

Your thoughts, emotions, and intent form a *micro-universe*. Shape that, and reality—and your reaction to it—shifts accordingly. Hermeticism supplies the "operating system": seven cosmic principles, planetary correspondences, and mental alchemy.

The Seven Principles in Plain Speech

1. **Mentalism** – Everything starts as an idea. *Practice*: spend 1 minute visualising today's best outcome before getting out of bed.
2. **Correspondence** – Patterns repeat across scales. *Practice*: note how your breath rate syncs with a friend's during calm conversation.
3. **Vibration** – Nothing is static; energy moves. *Practice*: clap slowly then quickly—feel the mood change.
4. **Polarity** – Opposites are two ends of one thing. *Practice*: list ways worry ⇄ excitement share the same energy.
5. **Rhythm** – Ups and downs are natural. *Practice*: track your alertness through the day, plan tasks to ride the peaks.
6. **Cause & Effect** – Nothing "just happens." *Practice*: trace a minor annoyance back through three prior choices.
7. **Gender (Generative Polarity)** – Everything has expressive / receptive aspects. *Practice*: ask which side a current project needs more of—action or incubation.

First Practical Working – *Planetary Candle Meditation* (15 min)

Each day of the week carries its own unique energy, traditionally linked to a celestial body and a guiding theme. You can deepen your connection to these rhythms by lighting a candle in a corresponding color and reflecting on that day's essence.

Monday, governed by the Moon, is a time for introspection. Light a **silver or white** candle to tune into your **intuition and dreams**.
Tuesday is ruled by fiery Mars—ignite a **red** candle to call in **courage and momentum** for the days ahead.
Wednesday belongs to Mercury, the planet of thought and expression. A **yellow** candle will support **study, learning, and communication**.
Thursday, under Jupiter's expansive influence, is perfect for focusing on **growth and good fortune**. Burn a **royal blue** candle to align with these energies.
Friday, sacred to Venus, is a day to celebrate the heart. A **green or pink** candle can invite **love, beauty, and harmony**.
Saturday is Saturn's day, ideal for setting **boundaries and embracing discipline**. A **black** candle provides grounding and structure.
And finally, **Sunday** shines with the Sun's golden light—illuminate a **gold** candle to boost your **vitality, confidence, and sense of purpose**.

1. Choose the day's candle colour.
2. Light it, state one **inner** goal ("clarify my thesis").
3. State one **outer** echo ("finish draft outline").
4. Gaze into the flame for 5 breaths, seeing the two merge.

5. Snuff the candle; step straight into a tiny related action (open document, draft one paragraph).

Common Pitfalls & Safeguards

- **Analysis Paralysis** – Correspondences can rabbit-hole. Pick *one* link (colour / planet / herb) per spell until fluent.
- **Cosmic Blame-Shift** – Retrogrades don't *make* you fail; they highlight issues. Use them to refine, not resign.
- **Spiritual Bypass** – Inner alchemy supports, not replaces, therapy or hard skills. Balance meditation with real-world work.

Folk Magic of Hearth & Hedge

"Use what's at hand; speak from the heart"

Core Idea

For millennia, everyday people—cunning-folk, granny-witches, root-workers—turned pantry goods and common tools into charms for health, luck, and protection. The magic lies as much in *storytelling* and *intentional use* as in exotic ingredients.

Starter Household Materia & Uses

- **Salt** – Purification; sprinkle a pinch counter-clockwise around a room to clear argument residue.
- **Iron Nail / Horseshoe** – Wards off the Evil Eye; place above door with points downward to "drain" malice.
- **Basil Leaves** – Draws prosperity; tuck three fresh leaves into your wallet every new moon.

- **Red Thread** – Binding & protection; knot nine times around a child's button to guard against nightmares.
- **Bay Leaf** – Wish magic; write desire on leaf, burn safely, scatter ash outside so wind carries it.

Five-Minute "Threshold Sweep" (weekly)

1. **Broom Pass** – Sweep from the back of the house straight out the front door while murmuring: "Out with the stale, in with the hale."
2. **Sun Water Flick** – Keep a jar of water charged on a sunny windowsill. After sweeping, dip fingers and flick droplets across doorway.
3. **Blessing Breath** – Exhale once across the threshold: picture a luminous veil sealing the entrance.

Rhythm of the Seasons

Spring – The Cleansing Breath of Beginnings

As the earth awakens, so too does the spirit. In olden times, people would sweep their homes with birch twigs to clear away the stale energy of winter. Today, you might begin your spring by cleansing your digital space—deleting one hundred old emails while whispering a simple mantra of renewal. Let each deletion be a clearing of old thoughts, making room for new growth.

Summer – The Sun's Embrace of Joy

Summer was once the season to gather St. John's Wort at noon, capturing the height of the sun's healing energy. In modern times, you might brew a lemon balm sun tea instead. As the herbs steep beneath the golden light, stir in your intentions for joy and vitality. Drink slowly, and let each sip radiate warmth through your soul.

Autumn – The Harvest of Heart and Health

Apples have long been used in charms for love and wellness. In your own kitchen, slice fresh apples and dust them with cinnamon. As they bake, infuse them with whispered blessings—for health, for love, for protection. With each bite, you're not just feeding your body, but nurturing your spirit as well.

Winter – The Ancestors' Warmth and Wisdom

When the cold bites and darkness deepens, witches once simmered spices to drive away sickness and gloom. Today, you might slow-cook onions and garlic, letting the fragrant steam rise and curl like ancestral breath. Inhale deeply. Give thanks to those who came before you, and feel their protection wrap around your home.

Common Pitfalls & Safeguards

- **Ingredient Snobbery** – Power isn't in rarity. A penny & intention beats imported resin you don't connect with.
- **Fear-Based Lore** – Some old charms threaten harm. Re-frame them toward *protect & heal*, not "return curse thrice."
- **Record-Keeping Neglect** – Folk magic thrives on observation. Keep a simple notebook: *date* • *what you did* • *what happened*. Patterns teach faster than any teacher.

Weaving the Three Streams Together

1. **Morning** – Wiccan root: ground & thank the Earth while opening curtains.
2. **Mid-day Task** – Hermetic branch: match work session to planetary hour for focus.
3. **Evening Home Care** – Folk blossom: simmer a cleansing pot of citrus peels & rosemary while sweeping arguments away.

With these practices, even a total beginner can **feel** the currents at work on Day One—and grow skill and subtlety as experience deepens. Remember: *start small, start sincere, and let respect guide every gesture.*

ILLUMINATING THE PATH – PRINCIPLES AND ETHICS

Magic is a language of the soul, an ancient art that reflects the deepest layers of our intention. To practice **White Magic** responsibly, we first ground ourselves in **ethical principles**— commitments to compassion, honesty, humility, and respect for all beings.

The Moral Compass of White Magic

1. **Harm None:** A core tenet borrowed from Wiccan tradition, reminding us that the ultimate aim of any spell or ritual is healing, help, or self-improvement—never compulsion or malice.
2. **Consent and Free Will:** Whenever possible, ask permission before performing magic for others. Honor their journey and autonomy.
3. **Integrity in Word and Deed:** Magic is more than incantations; it is a way of living. Your daily actions, speech, and thoughts ripple outward, affecting the world.
4. **Responsibility and Reflection:** Accept responsibility for your spells. If unintended consequences arise, reflect on what might have gone awry and how you can rectify or learn from the situation.

By weaving these principles into your practice, you ensure that your growing power aligns with love and light, benefiting both yourself and the wider cosmos.

CIRCLE OF VIRTUOUS ACCORD (RITUAL)

Purpose: Create a **sacred circle** in which you vow to uphold compassion, wisdom, and respect for free will. This is an **oath** that anchors your magical journey in **unshakeable integrity**.

When to Use: at the very start of your practice or whenever moral clarity feels shaky.

Difficulty: ★☆☆ (ideal for beginners).

Time Required: ≈ 20 minutes.

Outcome: plants a firm ethical compass that you can recall before every future spell.

Materials

- **Four small candles** (one for each element):
    - Earth (green or brown candle),
    - Air (yellow or white candle),
    - Fire (red or orange candle),
    - Water (blue candle).

    If you only have white candles, label them or place them in the cardinal directions.

- **One central white or gold candle** to represent Spirit.
- A **bowl of purified water** (you can use bottled water, or briefly bless tap water).
- A **pinch of salt**.
- A **paper** on which you have written your personal codes or a short prayer of ethical dedication.
- (Optional) **Incense** for atmosphere and cleansing.

Steps

1. **Purify the Space**

- Light incense or gently sprinkle salt water around the room.
- Say:

> *"I cleanse this place with sacred breath and sanctified water; let no ill or stray intent remain."*

2. Position the Candles
- Place the four elemental candles at the four cardinal directions (East, South, West, North).
- In the center, set the white/gold candle.

3. Mix Water and Salt
- Combine a pinch of salt into the bowl of water.
- Hold your hand over it, intoning:

> **Longer Invocation Example**
> "Holy currents of Earth and Sea,
> I ask you now to cleanse and free
> This water from all traces dark,
> That it may serve the Light's own spark.
> By the wave's gentle grace and ancient ground,
> Let purity in this bowl be found."

4. Cast the Circle
- Begin at the East. Light the East candle, saying:

> "I call upon the winds of the East:
> Carry clarity and truth within this rite.
> May thought be pure, words be honest,
> And illusions be swept away by your breeze."

- Move to the South:

"I call upon the fires of the South:
Ignite my passion for goodness,
Burn away fear and hesitation,
And shine courage into this circle."

- Move West:

    "I call upon the waters of the West:
    Cleanse my emotions, flow with empathy.
    Let compassion surge in every tide,
    And heal all who enter this circle."

- Move North:

    "I call upon the earth of the North:
    Ground my spirit in wisdom and stability.
    May endurance and strength be my allies,
    Steady as the mountain's ancient bones."

- Return to the center. Light the central candle:

    "I call upon Spirit, the unifying flame:
    Weave together these elements
    And guide my oath in the radiance of truth.
    From the infinite spark of creation,
    Let this circle be sanctified."

5. **State Your Ethics Aloud**
    - Read your written vows or say them from memory. For example:

        "I vow to practice magic in the name of healing,

with harm to none and respect for all.
I honor consent and free will,
And I accept the responsibility my power
entails."

6. Bless Yourself with the Water
- Dip your fingertips in the salted water.
- Touch your forehead, heart, and hands, saying:

"With this water, I cleanse my mind,
open my heart, and sanctify my hands,
that I may always act in love."

7. Moment of Reflection
- Stand or sit quietly in the circle, feeling the energies.
- You may close your eyes and sense each element flowing into your aura.

8. Seal the Circle
- Extinguish or leave the candles as you choose (if they're small enough, let them burn safely).
- If you close the circle now, walk counter-clockwise, thanking each elemental quarter in reverse order.
- End by saying:

"The circle opens, yet remains unbroken,
For in my heart, these vows are spoken."

This **Circle of Virtuous Accord** establishes an unassailable foundation for your craft. In times of moral doubt or temptation, recall this moment to realign yourself with the **Light** you pledged to serve.

Consecration of Sincere Purpose (Spell)

Objective: Purify your **inner motivations** so that every spell, word, or deed arises from a place of sincerity and goodwill. This extended version includes a **longer prayer** to immerse you more deeply in the energy of purification.

When to Use: before launching a new magical project or making a major life decision.

Difficulty: ★☆☆.

Time Required: ≈ 15 minutes.

Outcome: purifies motivation and aligns thought, speech, and deed.

Materials

- A **white candle** (for purity).
- A **small bowl of water**.
- A **handful of fresh or dried rosemary** (or sage).
- A pinch of **salt**.

Steps

1. **Create the Sacred Atmosphere**
    - Dim the lights, light incense if you wish.
    - Place the white candle at the center of your working area.
2. **Infuse the Water**

- Mix rosemary and salt into the water. Stir slowly **clockwise**, chanting:

> **Extended Prayer**
> "O Spirit of the Cleansing Waters,
> Flow through me with healing grace.
> From ancient springs to final seas,
> Dissolve all falsehood in your embrace.
> May each droplet shine with truth,
> Reflecting the best I yearn to be."

3. **Light the Candle**
   - As it flares, speak:

> "White Flame of Clarity,
> Glow steadfast and bright;
> May your purity guide me now,
> Banishing shadows and doubt from my sight."

4. **Anoint Yourself**
   - Dip your fingers in the rosemary-salt water.
   - Touch your forehead (for clear thought), lips or throat (for honest speech), heart (for compassion), and hands (for righteous action).
   - Each time, recite:

> "By water and flame, I consecrate my purpose."

5. **Prayer of Sincerity**
   - Close your eyes, place one hand over your heart.
   - Speak from the soul:

> "Divine Source, watch over my intentions.
> Let me speak with kindness,
> act with fairness,
> and hold compassion in every breath.
> May my magic serve the greater good,
> and may I walk in the honest light of my own spirit."

6. **Visualize Light**
   - Imagine a **column of pure white light** descending, passing through the candle flame, then into you.
   - Sense your entire aura brightening, free of heaviness or malice.
7. **Completion**
   - Extinguish the candle or let it burn safely for a while.
   - Dispose of or pour the water outside with gratitude, returning the energy to the Earth.
   - You might end by saying:

   > "My thoughts shine clear, my words ring true; sincerity grows in all that I do."

By investing **longer invocations** and heartfelt prayer, you deepen your **emotional and spiritual alignment** with the vow to practice White Magic for benevolent ends.

VOW OF THE RADIANT PATH (RITUAL)

Purpose: A simple yet profound ceremony to **renew** your commitment to the Light whenever you feel the need—be it at the start of a season or after you've overcome a personal trial.

When to Use: at seasonal milestones or after overcoming a personal trial.

Difficulty: ★☆☆.

Time Required: ≈ 10 minutes.

Outcome: renews your commitment to benevolence and inner light.

Materials

- **One white or gold candle**.
- A **small mirror** or reflective surface.
- (Optional) **Bell** or **chime**.

Steps

1. **Quiet Preparation**
   - Find a peaceful moment at dawn or dusk, times of transition that symbolize renewal.
   - Set the candle before the mirror so the flame will reflect.
2. **Ring the Bell (Optional)**
   - If you have a bell, ring it gently three times, each peal echoing an invitation to the divine presence.
3. **Light the Candle**
   - Gaze into the mirror where the flame is reflected.
   - Breathe slowly, letting your mind empty of daily cares.
4. **Extended Prayer to the Light**
   - Cup your hands as though holding the glow of the flame, and speak at length:

"Infinite Light, luminous Heart of the cosmos,
I call upon Your radiance to guide my path.
As the candle's glow burns away the dark,
May my spirit stand in purest truth.
Let my words be honest, my actions just,
And my dreams aligned with compassion.
Should I stray from kindness, draw me back
To the warmth of Your everlasting grace.
May this oath be etched upon my heart,
So that I walk forever in Your radiance."

5. **Oath Declaration**
   - Now, speak your vow in your own words. Example:

   "I pledge myself anew to this radiant path,
   guided by love, ever mindful of others' freedom.
   I vow to shine a gentle light wherever I tread,
   and to learn from every shadow I encounter."

6. **Absorb the Reflection**
   - Look into the mirror. Imagine you are drinking in the candle's aura, which merges with your own reflection.

7. **Seal the Ritual**
   - Blow out the candle (or snuff it), saying:

   "The outer flame rests, the inner flame endures—
   So mote it be, now and always."

   - If used, ring the bell once more in gratitude.

This vow resonates as a **spiritual anchor**, reminding you that even in mundane settings, you carry within you a **spark of divine luminosity**.

QUADRIVIUM OF SACRED WINDS (SPELL)

Aim: Request and receive **elemental blessings** from the four cardinal directions to restore balance and harmony in your life.

When to Use: at the start of a new chapter, or whenever you feel scattered, overwhelmed, or out of sync with nature's rhythm.

Difficulty: ★☆☆ (ideal for beginners).

Time Required: ≈ 15 minutes.

Outcome: attunes you to the elemental forces of Earth, Air, Fire, and Water, restoring internal balance and planting an enduring sense of harmony to carry into every future spell.

Steps

1. **Stand at Center**
   - If possible, do this outdoors or in a room with enough space to turn freely.
   - Close your eyes, ground yourself with slow breaths.
2. **Face East—Invocation of Air**
   - Extend your arms outward, feeling the intangible presence of wind.
   - Recite a **long invocation**:

> "Spirits of the East, gentle Air and dancing Breeze,
> Stir my thoughts to clarity, whisper insight to my mind.
> Sweep away doubt, carry new ideas on your wings.
> In this place, I welcome your quicksilver grace."

3. **Turn South—Invocation of Fire**
   - Place your hands over your solar plexus (the seat of will).
   - Speak your prayer:

     > "Flames of the South, radiant Fire,
     > Ignite my courage and passion for good.
     > Burn through stagnation, purify my desires.
     > Let the spark of creation blaze within me."

4. **Turn West—Invocation of Water**
   - With palms open, face the West.
   - Offer your plea:

     > "Waters of the West, fluid and deep,
     > Cleanse my heart, heal my wounds.
     > May empathy flow through me like a gentle river,
     > And compassion bathe every shore of my being."

5. **Turn North—Invocation of Earth**
   - Stomp lightly or place your hands on the ground.
   - Voice your prayer:

"Earth of the North, unwavering and strong,
Grant me stability and steadfast roots.
May I stand firm in life's storms,
And yield abundance to all who share my
path."

6. **Return to Center—Spirit**
   o Lift your arms upward or place them over your
     heart.
   o Say:

   "Source of Spirit, weaving all elements as
   one,
   Infuse me now with unity and divine
   connection.
   As above, so below; as within, so without."

7. **Collective Blessing**
   o Close your eyes and envision streams of light from
     each direction converging in your heart.
   o Feel yourself enveloped by the synergy of Earth,
     Air, Fire, Water, and Spirit.
8. **Seal**
   o Whisper: *"In gratitude, I receive these blessings.
     May harmony reign within and without. So mote it
     be."*

The **Quadrivium of Sacred Winds** not only fortifies you with
elemental gifts but also recalibrates you to **universal
rhythms**, ensuring you move forward in **equilibrium**.

FORTUNE'S BENEFIC PURSE (CHARM)

Function: A **small pouch** filled with tokens of positivity and good will. Keeping it close serves as a reminder to act kindly and to trust that generosity will return to you in kind.

When to Use: at the start of a generosity practice, before gifting or charity, or whenever you want to align with the energy of abundance and goodwill.

Difficulty: ★☆☆ (ideal for beginners)

Time Required: 15 minutes (depending on pace and depth of focus)

Outcome: creates a physical charm that anchors you in kindness, amplifies generous intentions, and attracts blessings through karmic reciprocity.

Assembly & Invocation

1. **Select Your Materials**
   - A **fabric pouch** (white, gold, or light green).
   - **Three coins** (pennies or any currency).
   - A pinch of **basil or mint** (herbs known for luck and prosperity).
   - A small **clear quartz** (to amplify good intentions).
   - A pinch of **salt** (for purity).
2. **Cleanse & Consecrate**
   - Pass each item through the smoke of incense or wave it around a lit white candle.
   - Recite:

"May these tokens bear no ill,
but shine with blessings bright.
I cleanse them in the name of good,
and fill them with benevolent might."

3. **Place Items in the Pouch**
   o Add the coins, saying:

   > "Coins for the flow of fortune, thrice returned
   > in kindly ways."

   o Add the basil or mint:

   > "Green leaves of luck, fresh and alive,
   > let good will bloom wherever I strive."

   o Add the quartz:

   > "Crystal of clarity, amplify my pure intention."

   o Sprinkle salt:

   > "Salt of Earth, preserve the goodness stored
   > herein."

4. **Tie & Charge**
   o Tie or knot the pouch.
   o Hold it in your hands, focusing on **good karma**.
   o Speak a longer prayer or poem, for instance:

   > "By the radiance of a giving heart,
   > and the wisdom of universal law,
   > I offer kindness freely, free of fear or flaw.

May each small act of love return in beams of grace,
welcoming blessings into the still, sacred heart of my everyday life.
What I sow, let me surely reap, thrice multiplied from realms so deep.
So mote it be."

5. **Placement**
    - Carry the pouch in your pocket or bag, or hang it where you'll see it daily.
    - Whenever you notice it, remember your commitment to doing good and trust in the **benefic** flow of the universe.

By embracing these expanded prayers, incantations, and steps, you ensure that the principles described here form a strong moral and energetic foundation. The spells are designed to purify, uplift, and align your will with the highest good, setting a tone of compassion and mindfulness for all the chapters that follow.

SACRED SPACES & TOOLS OF THE CRAFT

Once your ethical compass is set, the next key step is shaping a **physical and energetic environment** that nurtures your evolving practice. A **dedicated space**—however large or small—anchors your magic in the everyday world. Similarly, well-chosen and consecrated tools become extensions of your will.

The Nature of a Sacred Space

Think of your **sacred space** as a **dimensional crossroads** where the mundane dissolves, and the subtle realms glow more clearly. It may be a corner of your living room or a hidden nook in your garden. By sanctifying it, you transform it into a **haven** for ritual and introspection—a place where cosmic energy and personal intention harmonize.

SANCTUM ANOINTMENT RITE (RITUAL)

Purpose: To bless and activate your **altar**—the heart of your magical work.

When to Use: whenever your emotions feel out of balance or before important events.

Difficulty: ★★☆.

Time Required: ≈ 15 minutes.

Outcome: restores elemental harmony and centers your aura.

Materials

- A **table**, **shelf**, or **chest** that will serve as your altar.
- **Altar cloth** (optional).
- **Incense** (for Air).
- A small bowl of **water** (for Water).
- A small **candle** (for Fire).
- A small dish of **salt** or a **stone** (for Earth).
- One **larger candle** in white or gold to represent Spirit.

Steps

1. **Physical Cleansing**
   o Wipe down or wash the altar surface.
   o Lay the altar cloth if using.
2. **Arrange the Elements**
   o Place salt/stone to represent Earth in the north corner of the altar.
   o Place the incense or a feather to represent Air in the east corner.
   o Place the candle for Fire in the south corner.
   o Place the bowl of water in the west corner.
3. **Center Candle**
   o In the middle, place the white/gold candle for Spirit.
4. **Anoint the Altar**
   o Light the small candle (Fire) and pass it gently in a circle over the altar.
   o As you do, recite:

> "I awaken this sanctum with Fire's spark,
> that it may glow with life and devotion."

   o Next, sprinkle a few drops of water on the surface:

"By Water's grace, let this altar be pure and flowing."

- Wave the incense (or feather) over it:

    "By Air's breath, let clear thought and aspiration fill this space."

- Touch the salt or stone to each corner:

    "By Earth's firm embrace, may this place be stable and strong."

5. **Call on Spirit**
    - Light the central candle:

        Extended Invocation
        "Spirit, Heart of creation,
        Descend upon this holy table.
        Infuse it with the radiance of cosmic unity,
        That all who come here find solace and strength.
        May the words spoken here echo with truth,
        And the silence hold the whisper of the Divine."

6. **Moment of Stillness**
    - Close your eyes, rest your palms on the altar.
    - Sense any shift in energy—a gentle hum or a feeling of welcome.

7. **Consecration Seal**
    - Say:

"This altar stands as a bridge between worlds;
a meeting place of Earth and Sky,
of mortal heart and eternal spirit.
Blessed be this sanctum,
now and always."

8. **Maintenance**
    o Extinguish or let the candles burn safely.
    o Keep your altar clean and rearrange items as your practice evolves.

Tools as Extensions of Self

The implements of the Craft—athame, wand, chalice, crystals—carry profound symbolism. The **athame** often represents Air or Fire, slicing through illusions or focusing will. The **wand** channels energy fluidly, the **chalice** receives and nurtures, and crystals amplify or balance. Over time, each tool becomes **attuned** to your spirit, intensifying your magic.

INSTRUMENTS OF SACRED PURPOSE (RITUAL)

Goal: To **cleanse** and **imbue** a magical tool with your personal vibration, ensuring it resonates with your ethical stance and spiritual calling.

When to Use: when acquiring a new magical tool or whenever an existing one feels energetically misaligned or neglected.

Difficulty: ★☆☆ (ideal for beginners)

Time Required: 10 minutes

Outcome: forges a personal bond between you and your magical tool, grounding it in your spiritual values and ensuring it serves your highest intentions moving forward.

Materials

- The **tool** (athame, wand, chalice, mortar and pestle, etc.).
- **Four elemental representations** as before: a dish of salt (Earth), a feather/incense (Air), a lit candle (Fire), and a small bowl of water (Water).
- (Optional) **Oil** to anoint the tool.

Ritual Steps

1. **Center Yourself**
   - Stand or sit with the tool in your hands.
   - Inhale slowly, exhale any tension.
2. **Call Upon Each Element**
   - Present the tool to the salt, saying:

     "Earth, in your steadfastness, ground this tool in truth.
     Let it bear no heaviness of past misdeeds."

   - Pass it above the candle flame (cautiously):

     "Fire, in your purifying heat, burn away all disharmony.
     Ignite a noble purpose within this instrument."

   - Wave it through incense smoke or by a feather:

"Air, in your clarity, blow fresh life into this tool.
Carry away any remnants of confusion."

- Sprinkle water on it:

"Water, in your healing current, cleanse and bless this vessel.
Wash away all that is stagnant."

3. Oil Anointing (Optional)
- Dab your fingertips with oil.
- Trace a symbol (like a pentacle, cross, or personal sigil) on the tool:

"I anoint you under the watch of Spirit—
Serve the Light, guided by pure intention."

4. Longer Consecration Prayer
- Lift the tool toward the sky or hold it over your heart:

"Cosmic Source, bestow your grace
On this humble instrument I raise.
May it channel my will with honesty,
May it echo my vow of harm to none.
In times of doubt, let it remind me
Of the promise I made when I first began.
Let it be a beacon in shadowed hours,
A conductor of hope when light is scarce."

5. Envision Unity
- Envision a gentle white-gold glow enveloping the tool.

- Sense a connection forming between you and it—a **thread of energy** that hums with cooperation.

6. **Close**
   - Thank each element.
   - Conclude with a phrase like:

     "Consecrated and sealed, so let it be."

7. **Storage**
   - Store or display the tool in a sacred place, ensuring it remains free from casual handling if possible.

HEARTH-WARD CLEANSING (SPELL)

Purpose: To **cleanse** your home of negativity and establish a **protective ward** against future intrusions.

When to Use: during seasonal transitions, after emotional upheaval, or anytime your home feels energetically heavy or vulnerable.

Difficulty: ★☆☆ (ideal for beginners)

Time Required: 15–30 minutes, depending on the size of your space and how slowly you move through the house

Outcome: clears lingering negativity from your space and establishes a gentle but firm ward of protection, creating a safe, sacred atmosphere for all who dwell within.

Materials

- A **bowl of water**.
- A pinch of **salt**.
- A few **protective herbs** (e.g., rosemary, thyme, lavender).
- A **white candle**.
- (Optional) **Broom** or **besom** for a folk-inspired floor sweep.

Method

1. **Combine & Bless**
   - In your chosen sacred area (possibly your newly sanctified altar), add salt and herbs to the water.
   - Stir clockwise while reciting:

     "From leaf and salt, from water's deep,
     gather purifying power to banish what creeps.
     Ward this home with watchful grace,
     let no ill remain in this space."

2. **Light the White Candle**
   - Place it near the bowl.
   - Speak:

     "Candle of cleansing, flame of hope,
     burn away shadows, help us cope.
     Shine bright in every corner and hall,
     so negativity has no hold at all."

3. **House Tour**
   - Dip your fingertips in the water. Flick droplets around doorways, windows, corners.
   - If using a broom, gently sweep from the back of each room toward the door.
   - Each time, say a line like:

> "Be gone all strife, be gone all harm—
> only blessings may here take form."

4. **Focus on Entrances**
    - Spend extra time at the front door.
    - Make a small cross or spiral with the water on the threshold:

    > "At this portal, I draw a line—
    > negativity, stay out; only goodwill may shine."

5. **Return to the Candle**
    - Let it burn as you visualize your home glowing with a **soft, protective radiance**.
6. **Dispose or Store Water**
    - You may pour the leftover water outside to carry away negativity.
    - Or, if you prefer, bottle some of it as "cleansing water" for future quick purifications.
7. **Gratitude**
    - Extinguish the candle (or let it burn if safe).
    - Whisper a final thanks:

    > "Guardians seen and unseen,
    > I thank you for your steadfast shield.
    > May peace reign and hearts be light,
    > within these walls by day and night."

GUARDIAN OF THE THRESHOLD (CHARM)

Function: Craft a **talisman** that hangs near your main entry, warding off malevolent influences and blessing those who enter with **peaceful energy**.

When to Use: when moving into a new home, after emotional disturbances, or anytime your entryway feels energetically vulnerable or unguarded.

Difficulty: ★☆☆ (ideal for beginners)

Time Required: 10–15 minutes, depending on the level of focus and any additional embellishments

Outcome: creates a protective talisman that shields your entryway, repels negativity, and blesses all who cross your threshold with calm, respectful energy.

Steps

1. **Pouch Creation**
   - Gather a small cloth pouch or square of fabric.
   - Place a pinch of salt, protective herbs (like basil, bay leaf, or rue), and a tiny crystal (obsidian, onyx, or black tourmaline) inside.
2. **Extended Prayer**
   - Hold the open pouch to your heart, saying:

     "Spirit of safety, guardian of doorways,
     I call upon you to dwell in this humble charm.
     Ward off ill will, reflect malice back to the

void,
Let harmony greet all who step across the threshold.
Bless friend and stranger alike
with respect and kindness abiding."

3. **Seal**
    - Tie the pouch with a ribbon or cord.
    - As you knot it, speak:

        "By knot of one, this charm's begun;
        by knot of two, its power is true;
        by knot of three, it protects for me."

4. **Placement**
    - Hang it near the door or above the lintel.
    - If you prefer subtlety, place it behind a decoration or inside a door wreath.
5. **Periodic Renewal**
    - Once a month or so, anoint it with a drop of essential oil (e.g., frankincense) or lightly pass it through cleansing incense.

With your **altar awakened**, **tools consecrated**, **home purified**, and a **threshold charm** guarding the entrance, you have laid a strong physical and energetic foundation. This sets the stage for deeper explorations of **protection, purification, elemental allies, and beyond**, which we continue in the next chapter.

SPELLS OF PROTECTION AND PURIFICATION

No journey is without its shadows. Though the path of White Magic strives for healing and love, it also recognizes the importance of **self-defense** and **purity**. In this chapter, we delve into a range of spells and rituals that **shield**, **cleanse**, and **banish** negativity. Extending these spells with fuller invocations will deepen your confidence and clarity.

The Nature of Protective Magic

To protect is not to attack—it is to stand firm, respecting your own space and wholeness. When faced with malice, you can reflect or neutralize it without inflicting harm. Similarly, purification is an act of **restoration**—returning your personal or environmental energy to an unburdened state.

AEGIS OF THE ELEMENTAL QUADRANT (SPELL)

Purpose: Raise a **comprehensive shield** around a room, home, or personal space by uniting Earth, Air, Fire, and Water into a protective ring.

When to Use: before performing deep magical work, after emotional disruption in a space, or when establishing a long-term protective boundary in your sacred area.

Difficulty: ★☆☆ (ideal for beginners)

Time Required: 20–30 minutes, especially if you move mindfully and allow time to fully connect with each elemental invocation

Outcome: weaves Earth, Air, Fire, and Water into a unified elemental shield, forming a powerful energetic dome of protection around the space that can be sustained or refreshed over time.

Materials

- Four candles in elemental colors (Green/Brown for Earth, Yellow for Air, Red/Orange for Fire, Blue for Water) or simply four white candles labeled for each element.
- (Optional) A **center candle** to represent Spirit.

Method

1. **Position Candles**
   - Place them in the cardinal directions around the area you wish to shield.
2. **Invocations**
   - Move to the East candle, lighting it:

      Lengthy Prayer
      "I call upon the sylphs and gentle breezes of the East,
      Guardians of clarity and swift deliverance.
      Wrap this circle in airy currents,
      that no foul whisper or trickery may penetrate."

   - South candle:

      "I call upon the salamanders and bright flames of the South,
      Guardians of will and purging light.

Ignite this circle with fervent protection,
that malice be scorched into harmless ash."

- West candle:

    "I call upon the undines and flowing tides of the West,
    Guardians of compassion and cleansing water.
    Wash this circle of all discord,
    letting only healing currents remain."

- North candle:

    "I call upon the gnomes and fertile earth of the North,
    Guardians of stability and resilience.
    Root this circle in unwavering might,
    repelling all that is corrosive or unkind."

3. **Encircle with Energy**
    - Stand at the center, or walk the perimeter imagining lines of light connecting the four candles.
    - If using a center candle for Spirit, light it last:

        "Spirit, vessel of unity,
        weave these four into one unbreakable shield.
        May no harm or ill intent sustain itself within."

4. **Feel the Shield**
    - Close your eyes, sense a **dome of energy** forming.

- Breathe in the combined essence of the elements, exhaling any fear.

5. **Duration**
   - You can keep the circle for a single ritual or designate it as a **long-term ward**. In the latter case, you might restate the protective intention each day or each week.

6. **Thank and Dismiss (if temporary)**
   - Extinguish the candles in reverse order when you wish to end it, thanking each direction.
   - "Stay if you will, go if you must. With gratitude, we part in trust."

SPECULUM SANCTUS DEFLECTORIUM (CHARM)

Aim: A mirror-based **reflective charm** that repels harmful energies. Longer invocations help you connect deeply with the concept of reflection as both defense and clarity.

When to Use: when you sense yourself absorbing negativity, before entering emotionally charged spaces, or to protect your home or energy field from external harm.

Difficulty: ★☆☆ (ideal for beginners)

Time Required: 15–25 minutes, especially if taking time for cleansing, invocation, and energy visualization

Outcome: creates a reflective charm that repels negativity, neutralizes hostile intent, and strengthens your clarity and energetic boundaries through the sacred power of mirrored return.

Creation Steps

1. **Gather Materials**
    - A small mirror pendant or tiny reflective disc.
    - (Optional) A piece of black fabric or felt to cover the back.
    - A length of ribbon or chain to wear or hang the amulet.
2. **Cleansing**
    - Wipe the mirror with salt water.
    - Say:

        "Mirror of shining truth,
        be cleansed of all past images and residue.
        Stand ready to guard and reflect,
        absorbing none, releasing all."

3. **Inscription (Optional)**
    - If comfortable, inscribe a protective sigil or word (e.g., "PROTEGO") on the back with paint or a marker.
4. **Extended Invocation**
    - Light a candle. Hold the mirror so the flame reflects:

        "O Reflective Shield, vessel of light and return,
        I charge you to defend against all ill will.
        Should negativity approach,
        let it see only its own face
        and vanish into the formless void.
        By the mercy of the divine,
        I intend no harm, but simply stand in truth.

Let malice find no anchor here—
as I walk in the brilliance of kindly intentions."

5. **Empower with Breath**
   o Exhale gently onto the mirror's surface, visualizing a swirl of white energy settling into it.
6. **Wear or Place**
   o Attach the mirror to your chosen chain or ribbon.
   o Keep it near your heart if wearing, or hang it near a door or window if using as a household protector.
7. **Periodic Re-Cleansing**
   o Wipe the mirror with a damp cloth or pass it through incense occasionally, reaffirming the protective vow.

LUSTRATION OF SALT AND GREEN (RITUAL)

Purpose: To **purify** yourself, an object, or a space using the combined potency of salt and herbs, reinforced by prayerful recitations.

When to Use: after emotional heaviness, illness, conflict, or before sacred work to reset energy and welcome peace.

Difficulty: ★☆☆ (ideal for beginners)

Time Required: 20–30 minutes, especially if used for space-wide cleansing or full personal ritual bathing

Outcome: creates a sacred herbal wash that purifies the body, objects, or space of burdensome energy, replacing it with grounded clarity and Earth-blessed renewal.

Steps

1. **Herbal Selection**
   - Choose cleansing herbs: rosemary, thyme, sage, or any with strong purifying lore.
2. **Create the Wash**
   - Fill a **large bowl or cauldron** with warm water.
   - Stir in salt and the chosen herbs.
3. **Long Form Invocation**
   - As you stir clockwise, say:

     > "Gathered here are the gifts of Earth:
     > salt from ancient seas,
     > herbs from green fields and mountains.
     > I invoke the spirit of purification,
     > that all burdens be lifted
     > and all shadows dispelled.
     > By the grace of Earth's memory,
     > let this water become a balm to the weary
     > and a banisher of all that weighs heavy."

4. **Application**
   - **Personal Cleansing:** Dip your hands or even bathe your feet in the water. You might gently pour it over your shoulders in a shower or bath.
   - **Object Cleansing:** Submerge the item if water-safe (like crystals, small tools), or lightly sprinkle it.
   - **Room Cleansing:** Walk through the area, flicking water droplets into corners, doorways, etc.
5. **Focus & Visualization**
   - Imagine **dark or murky energy** dissolving in the water's presence, replaced by a fresh, vibrant glow.
6. **Closing Prayer**

o   Finish with a heartfelt statement:

> "All that was heavy, now washed away.
> All that was stifling, now turned to airy grace.
> May this place (or person/object)
> stand renewed in the cradle of Earth's
> benevolence."

7. **Dispose or Store**
   o   If you sense negativity was washed away, pour the water outside or down the drain while envisioning it neutralized.
   o   You can keep a portion in a bottle for future quick touch-ups if it feels purely charged.

REFLECTIVE AEGIS OF SILVER (SPELL)

Goal: Erect a **larger-scale reflective barrier**—especially effective if you suspect sustained negative attention or psychic intrusion.

When to Use: during periods of psychic strain, spiritual harassment, or when sensing sustained negative attention from others (intentional or not).

Difficulty: ★☆☆ (ideal for beginners)

Time Required: 20–30 minutes, depending on depth of prayer, visualization, and setup

Outcome: establishes a reflective, non-aggressive shield that gently dissolves or returns harmful energies, aligning your space or aura with clarity, peace, and sacred self-containment.

Method

1. **Obtain a Medium Mirror**
   - Big enough to stand upright.
2. **Salt Barrier**
   - Sprinkle a **ring of salt** on the floor or table around where you will place the mirror.
3. **Candle Reflection**
   - Light a silver or white candle. Place it so the flame is reflected in the mirror.
   - Speak slowly:

     "I kindle this flame in the name of luminous defense.
     Let all shadows recoil from its brilliance.
     Mirror before me, become a shield—
     gleaming with silver so negativity must yield."

4. **Extended Prayer**
   - Close your eyes, resting a hand on the mirror's edge if safe:

     "O Guardian of Reflection,
     stand sentinel against dark intent.
     By the law of cosmic balance,
     I seek no vengeance but only peace.
     Let harmful thoughts be dissolved
     or turned back to their source as gentle lessons.

In the realm of shining truth,
no falsehood can endure."

5. **Visualization**
   o See a **silver dome** expanding outward from the
     mirror, encapsulating your home or personal aura.
   o Let it shimmer like the surface of a moonlit lake,
     calm yet impenetrable.
6. **Duration**
   o Some keep the mirror displayed as a constant ward,
     covering it with black cloth when not needed.
   o Others use it temporarily for crises—performing the
     ritual, then storing the mirror away.
7. **Gratitude**
   o Whisper a final thanks:

> "Shield of silver, I honor your vigilance.
> My heart stands firm in kindness and light,
> and your reflection ensures that malice
> finds no harbor in my domain."

Through these **protection and purification** spells, you
safeguard your personal energy and environment. Whether
forging a circle of elemental guardians or reflecting harm
away with silver mirrors, you stand in **calm strength**, aligned
with the principle that **defense need not breed aggression**.

ELEMENTAL ALLIES – EARTH, AIR, FIRE, WATER, SPIRIT

Nature is not silent. She speaks through wind and flame, stone and stream, and through the subtle shimmer that binds them all. These are the five sacred forces—Earth, Air, Fire, Water, and Spirit—revered since the earliest dawns of magic. They are not just symbols or metaphors. They are living presences, woven into the breath of the world and the beating of your heart.

In the Western esoteric traditions, these elements are not separate from us—they *are* us. They shape the ground we walk, the thoughts we think, the desires that burn in our chest, and the tears we shed in silence. To walk the path of White Magic is to listen, to learn, and ultimately, to *befriend* these elemental powers. When honored with love and intention, they respond—not as tools to be commanded, but as allies to be trusted.

Let this be your first initiation: a quiet meeting with the five sacred currents that form the very bones of magic.

Earth – *The Bone of the World* (Grounding, fertility, sustenance**)**

She is the stillness beneath your feet, the weight of truth, the cradle of seed and stone. Earth holds the memory of every footstep and every grave. She teaches patience, presence, and how to grow roots even in chaos. Through her, you find grounding, nourishment, and the strength to build what lasts. She whispers, *Be still. Be steady. Become.*

Air – *The Voice of the Invisible* (Intellect, inspiration, communication)

Air is the realm of thought and breath, of insight and communication. It stirs the mind like wind through leaves, carrying inspiration from unseen places. Air is how we dream, how we speak, how we listen—to ourselves, to others, to the quiet spaces between. It invites clarity, curiosity, and freedom. It says, *Open your mind. Let your thoughts take flight.*

Fire – *The Sacred Flame Within* (Willpower, transformation, passion)

Fire is transformation in its purest form. It is hunger and courage, destruction and rebirth. It burns away what no longer serves, lighting the path forward with fierce brilliance. Fire lives in your will, your passion, your ability to choose and to act. It demands honesty and dares you to be bold. It roars, *Change. Burn. Create.*

Water – *The Heart's Deep Knowing* (Emotion, intuition, healing)

Water is the healer and the keeper of emotion. It holds the tides of grief and love, of intuition and memory. Water teaches us to feel without drowning, to move without breaking, to listen to the currents beneath the surface. It is ritual, renewal, and the wisdom that flows in silence. It murmurs, *Feel deeply. Flow gently. Heal.*

Spirit (Aether) – *The Breath Between Worlds*

Spirit is the silent thread that connects all things—the unseen presence that animates, inspires, and unites. It cannot be held or measured, yet it sings through every spell, every prayer, every sacred act. Spirit is your connection to the

Divine, however you name it. It is what makes magic *magic*. It says only, *Remember who you are.*

VESSEL OF VERDANT PROSPERITY (EARTH RITUAL)

Purpose: To invoke **Earth's nurturing power** for growth in finances, creativity, or personal stability.

When to Use: at the beginning of a new creative or financial endeavor, when seeking stability, or during times of personal reinvention and grounded growth.

Difficulty: ★☆☆ (ideal for beginners)

Time Required: 20–25 minutes, with ongoing care as part of the magic's living nature

Outcome: nurtures your intentions for prosperity through Earth's fertile energy, creating a living vessel that holds and reflects your desires as they grow in the physical and spiritual world.

Steps

1. **Gather Materials**
   - A **small pot**, **fertile soil**, and **seeds** (could be actual plant seeds or symbolic objects).
   - A bit of **blessed water** (possibly from the Lustration ritual).
2. **Long Form Invocation to Earth**
   - Hold the pot of soil, speaking:

> "Blessed Earth, ancient mother of forests and fields,
> I honor your patience, your eternal cycle of birth and decay.
> In this soil, I plant the dream of my prosperity—
> Let it take root in your abundant heart,
> Growing strong through my honest labor and heartfelt intentions."

3. **Planting the Seed**
   - Place the seed(s) in the soil.
   - Drizzle water gently, saying:

   > "Water of life, awaken this seed,
   > Let my hopes flourish in both seen and unseen realms."

4. **Personal Devotion**
   - Cup your hands around the pot, visualizing **your desire** blossoming.
   - Name your goal: *"May I find stability in my career,"* or *"May my art thrive and inspire,"* etc.

5. **Ongoing Care**
   - Place the pot in a suitable spot (light, temperature). Water it as needed.
   - As the plant grows, reaffirm your intention. If you used a symbolic seed (like a crystal or charm), keep it in the soil for a week or so, then remove and place it on your altar.

WINDS OF INNER KNOWING (AIR SPELL)

Intent: Summon **Air's swift intellect** to clear mental fog, enhance communication, or spark new ideas.

When to Use: before studying, writing, public speaking, or any situation that calls for mental clarity, creative inspiration, or graceful communication.

Difficulty: ★☆☆ (ideal for beginners)

Time Required: 10–15 minutes, depending on the depth of your invocation and visualization

Outcome: calls upon the element of Air to lift mental fog, awaken intellect, and spark eloquence, leaving you energized, articulate, and mentally attuned.

Materials

- A **feather** (natural or decorative) to represent Air.
- (Optional) A **small bell** or **wind chime**.

Process

1. **Purify the Feather**
    - Pass it through incense smoke.
    - Whisper:

        "By the breath of ancient winds,
        be freed of past imprints,
        ready to carry clarity anew."

2. **Lengthy Invocation**
    - Stand facing East, feather in hand:

    > "O Air of the East, realm of dawn and new beginnings,
    > I greet your fresh breezes that stir the mind awake.
    > Sweep away the cobwebs of confusion, bestow your gift of eloquence and bright ideas.
    > Let my thoughts be swift, my words be kind, that I may speak truth in love and find solutions that uplift."

3. **Charge the Feather**
    - Gently wave it around your head, imagining a **soft wind** clearing mental blocks.
    - If you have a bell, ring it lightly to symbolize the gentle stir of Air.

4. **Usage**
    - Whenever you need clarity—before a test, important talk, or brainstorming—lightly brush your brow with the feather, reaffirming:

    > "Mind be clear, words sincere, by Air's bright grace I persevere."

THE HOLLOW FIRE ASCENSION (FIRE RITUAL)

Purpose: To call upon Fire's transformative power to release old patterns, emotions, or beliefs—making space for renewal and growth.

When to Use: during times of personal transformation, endings, or emotional release—especially when you feel ready to shed limiting beliefs or begin anew.

Difficulty: ★☆☆ (ideal for beginners)

Time Required: 15–25 minutes, depending on how much reflection, prayer, and energy you give to the fire and release process

Outcome: Emotional burdens or inner blockages are transmuted into fuel for courage, clarity, and renewal—symbolizing your rebirth from what no longer serves.

Materials

- A **red**, **orange**, or **gold candle**.
- A small slip of paper and a pen.
- A **fireproof dish** to catch ashes.

Ritual Steps

1. **Naming the Obstacle**
   - Write on paper what you wish to release (e.g., self-doubt, anger, fear).
2. **Lighting the Candle**
   - Carve or draw a phoenix symbol (or a simple flame design) into the candle.
   - Speak an **extended invocation**:

     "Spirits of Fire, radiant keepers of life's spark,
     Hear my call as I stand at the threshold of change.

> "Like the phoenix rising from its own ashes,
> Let me shed these worn-out burdens.
> Burn away illusions, devour my fears,
> and rekindle my courage and passion anew."

3. **Burning the Paper**
    - Carefully ignite the paper with the candle flame.
    - Drop it into the dish, visualizing **smoke** carrying away your obstacle.
4. **Self-Blessing**
    - Warm your hands near the candle (without burning yourself).
    - Imagine a gentle heat spreading through you, energizing your will to change.
    - Say:

    > "From ash to flame, from dark to light,
    > I embrace the Phoenix Rite."

5. **Completion**
    - Let the candle burn safely for a while or extinguish it.
    - Scatter the cooled ashes to the wind or bury them.

SELENIC TIDE PURIFICATION (WATER SPELL)

Aim: Merge the healing properties of **Water** with **lunar energy** for deep emotional cleansing.

When to Use: during a full or waxing moon, especially when emotions feel heavy, grief lingers, or your inner world needs calming clarity.

Difficulty: ★☆☆ (ideal for beginners)

Time Required: 30–60 minutes, depending on moon phase, soaking time, and how long you linger in stillness and release

Outcome: merges lunar and water energies to gently cleanse emotional residue, dissolve inner tension, and restore calm presence through the moon's soothing embrace.

Steps

1. **Moonlit Water**
   o   Under a waxing or full moon, set out a bowl of fresh water (or collected rainwater, if possible).
2. **Invocation to the Moon**
   o   Stand under the moonlight, hold the bowl:

> "Luna, silver guardian of night's gentle power,
> Reflect your grace into these waters.
> Wash over my heart's hidden sorrows,
> soothe my soul, bring calm to my waters within.
> May your reflection guide me to clarity."

3. **Adding Salt or Herbs (Optional)**
   o   If you like, sprinkle a pinch of salt or mild herbs (chamomile, for tranquility).
4. **Anointment**
   o   After an hour or so, bring the bowl indoors.
   o   Gently dip your fingers, anoint your brow, heart, and wrists.
   o   Feel the **cool lunar vibration** dissolving stress or old grief.

5. **Optional Soak**
   - You may add the moon-charged water to a bath for a full-body purification.
6. **Moon Gratitude**
   - Extinguish or blow a kiss to the moon, saying:

   "My gratitude for your soothing tide.
   In lunar hush, my spirit abides."

ETHEREAL CONFLUENCE BENEDICTION (SPIRIT RITUAL)

Objective: Attune to the **fifth element**, Spirit or Aether, the divine breath that unites Earth, Air, Fire, and Water.

When to Use: during moments of spiritual longing, before major magical workings, or when seeking a deeper connection to the divine thread that unites all elements.

Difficulty: ★☆☆ (ideal for beginners)

Time Required: 20–30 minutes, depending on how long you remain in silent communion or absorb the invocation's energy

Outcome: gently opens you to the presence of Spirit—the fifth element—awakening a sense of divine unity, inner peace, and soulful alignment with the cosmos.

Method

1. **Candle or Crystal**

- A **white or clear quartz crystal** can represent Spirit.
- Light a white candle next to it.

2. **Centering**
   - Sit comfortably, close your eyes.
   - Breathe slowly, imagining you are inhaling **pure light** into your heart.

3. **Long Invocation**
   - Place a hand over the crystal or candle flame (not too close):

> "Spirit of unity, boundless and free,
> Dwelling in stars and in the depths of me,
> I open my soul to your silent voice
> that whispers in wind, in flame, in ocean's rejoice.
> In Earth's gentle pulse, in Air's stirring breeze,
> in Fire's dancing glow, in Water's flowing ease—
> You are the current weaving them all.
> Join me now in synergy divine,
> bridging the mortal and cosmic design.
> Let me feel the presence of one universal love,
> that I may walk with grace below and blessings from above."

4. **Absorption of Light**
   - Visualize a **pillar of radiant energy** descending from above, merging with your aura.
   - Let yourself bask in a sense of **oneness**.

5. **Quiet Reflection**
   - Stay in silence for several minutes, simply listening.

- You may receive subtle insights or a peaceful emptiness.
6. **Gratitude & Return**
    - Thank Spirit for the communion.
    - Extinguish the candle, or let it burn safely.
    - Keep the crystal on your altar as a reminder of this connection.

By working with each element and honoring Spirit's unifying presence, you evolve a **holistic practice** that resonates with the intricate harmony of all living things. The more you **experience** the elements in direct ritual, the deeper your **relationship** with them grows—building a magical synergy that enriches every facet of your craft.

MOONLIGHT AND SUNFIRE – LUNAR & SOLAR MAGIC

The **celestial dance** of the moon and sun influences tides, seasons, and the very rhythm of life. Aligning magic with these forces amplifies spellwork, channels cyclical energy, and harmonizes personal growth with the cosmos. This chapter deepens your interplay with **lunar** and **solar** powers.

Lunar Phases & Their Influence

1. New Moon (Dark Moon)

Themes: *Reflection, new beginnings, subtle planting of intentions*

The New Moon is a time of stillness and potential. The sky is dark, a cosmic pause between cycles. This is the **seed stage**, where nothing is visible, but everything is possible. It's ideal for deep reflection, inner contemplation, and **setting quiet, soulful intentions** for what you wish to grow. These seeds may be emotional, spiritual, or physical—dreams not yet spoken, changes not yet begun.
Spells for: Beginnings, setting intentions, fertility, new ventures.

2. Waxing Moon

Themes: *Growth, attraction, building of power*

As the moon begins to grow in light, so too do our goals and desires. The Waxing Moon is the **momentum phase**, perfect for taking action and fueling your intentions. This is the time to focus on **attraction magic**, productivity, and expansion. Each night the moon shines a little brighter, reflecting the growth you're cultivating within and without.

Spells for: Abundance, love, success, drawing opportunities or people to you.

3. Full Moon

Themes: *High tide of energy, manifestation, celebration*

The Full Moon is the **climax of the lunar cycle**—a radiant spotlight in the sky. It's when the moon's energy is at its peak, magnifying emotions, intuition, and spiritual connection. This is the ideal time for **manifestation, gratitude, divination, and powerful spellwork**. It's also a time for celebration, illumination, and clarity. What was hidden can now be seen. *Spells for:* Power, protection, manifestation, divination, celebration, charging crystals/tools.

4. Waning Moon

Themes: *Releasing, banishing, letting go*

As the moon begins to shrink, so do the energies that no longer serve us. This phase is for **cleansing and release**—of habits, relationships, fears, or spiritual blockages. Think of it as a sacred decluttering. The waning moon invites us to clear the space we need in order to heal, rest, and prepare for renewal.
Spells for: Banishing, breaking bad habits, protection, cord-cutting, purification.

5. Dark Moon (just before New)

Themes: *Inner work, rest, transformation of shadows*

The Dark Moon—sometimes considered a distinct phase—is the final breath before the new cycle. It's a time of deep inner mystery, often associated with the Crone archetype. This is a moment for **shadow work**, for communing with your unconscious and confronting your fears or suppressed truths. It's the death before the rebirth, and it calls for **silence, solitude, and surrender**.
Spells for: Shadow work, deep healing, ancestral contact, spiritual detox, dreamwork.

DARKMOON GENESIS SPELL (NEW MOON)

Purpose: Harness the **subtle yet potent** energy of the new moon to initiate fresh starts.

When to Use: on the night of the new moon or within its first 24 hours—ideal for setting intentions related to beginnings, subtle transformation, and inner rebirth.

Difficulty: ★☆☆ (ideal for beginners)

Time Required: 15–25 minutes, depending on the time spent visualizing and connecting with the dark moon's quiet energy

Outcome: initiates a subtle yet powerful shift toward new beginnings by aligning your intention with the fertile stillness of the new moon, planting psychic seeds in the womb of night.

Steps

1. **Black or Dark Candle**

- Light it in a quiet, dim space.
- Speak:

> "Darkmoon cradle, womb of night,
> from your void all creation takes flight.
> I rest in your silent promise,
> sowing seeds of new possibility."

2. **Write the Intention**
   - On a slip of paper, describe what you wish to invoke in your life (e.g., a new job, spiritual insight).
3. **Planting the Seed**
   - Fold the paper.
   - If you have a small dish of earth or pot, bury it lightly. Otherwise, simply hold it.
4. **Long Invocation**
   - Kneel before the candle, reciting:

> "In the hush of this moonless sky,
> I plant the seeds of tomorrow.
> May they sprout with honesty and love,
> fed by cosmic wonder and guided by subtle grace.
> As the moon waxes, so too shall my vision grow,
> nurtured by patience and luminous hope."

5. **Visualize**
   - Imagine the candle's flame igniting **tiny sparks** of light within your folded paper or pot of earth—symbolizing the **dormant power** of your intention.
6. **Completion**
   - Extinguish the candle or let it burn partially.

- Keep the folded paper in a safe place or let it remain buried until you see the first crescent moon.

Lunar Apex Convergence (Full Moon Ritual)

Aim: Absorb the **peak power** of the full moon to **consecrate** tools, crystals, or your personal aura.

When to Use: on the night of the full moon to charge magical tools, heighten spiritual awareness, or realign your personal energy with lunar power.

Difficulty: ★☆☆ (ideal for beginners)

Time Required: 25–35 minutes, depending on how many items you're charging and how long you remain in communion with the moon

Outcome: fills tools, crystals, or your aura with the height of lunar energy—awakening clarity, strength, intuition, and luminous peace that carries into your daily magic and spirit.

Method

1. **Outside or Window**
    - If possible, perform under direct moonlight. Otherwise, near a window that catches the moon's rays.
2. **Create a Circle**
    - Outline a circle with small stones or just visualize a **luminous ring**.

3. Extended Full Moon Invocation
- Standing in the circle, arms raised:

> "Grandmother Moon, in your fullest bloom,
> shower this circle with silver serenity.
> Let your beams enliven these tools (or crystals),
> imbuing them with clarity, intuition, and strength.
> I open my heart to your glowing counsel,
> that I may reflect your radiant glow in my daily path.
> As the tide peaks, let my spirit rise,
> brimming with possibility and gentle might."

4. Charging Objects
- Place crystals, talismans, or your Book of Shadows in the circle.
- Visualize them **soaking** in moonlight.

5. Self-Anointment
- If you like, anoint your forehead with moon-charged water or oil.
- Affirm:

> "I, too, shine in the fullness of my being."

6. Quiet Communion
- Spend a few minutes just standing or sitting under the moon, sensing her calm luminescence filling you.

7. Close
- Thank the moon:

> "Mother of tides, your gift I cherish.
> Let these blessings remain as your cycle flows on."

8. **Store the Energy**
   - Collect your charged items.
   - If possible, leave them by a window overnight for an extra infusion.

TIDE OF THE SILVER CRESCENT (WAXING MOON SPELL)

Purpose: Draw positivity or desired outcomes into your life while the moon **increases** in visibility.

When to Use: during the waxing moon, especially when beginning a new goal, desire, or manifestation that you wish to grow in strength and visibility over time.

Difficulty: ★☆☆ (ideal for beginners)

Time Required: 10–20 minutes for the initial ritual, with optional 5–10 minute nightly renewals until the full moon

Outcome: gently draws your desire toward you as the moon grows, aligning your intention with the rhythm of natural expansion, hope, and becoming.

Steps

1. **Green or Gold Candle**

o Carve a symbol of what you wish to attract (money sign, heart, rune for success).

2. **Prayer to the Waxing Moon**
   o Light the candle, facing where the waxing moon would be:

> "Crescent Moon, bright with potential,
> as you grow in shining arcs,
> so may my dream find fertile ground.
> Pull my desire gently to me,
> the way you draw the tides.
> Let each passing night expand my hope,
> until fullness meets fulfillment."

3. **Visualize Growth**
   o Envision your goal **sprouting** like a seed, fed by lunar light.

4. **Incremental Ritual**
   o You can relight the candle each night until the full moon, repeating a short chant.

5. **Conclusion**
   o Extinguish or snuff the candle gently, saying:

> "With gratitude, I pause.
> May the moon carry my wish onward."

DIMINISHING SHADOWS INCANTATION (WANING MOON SPELL)

Aim: Let go of toxic relationships, habits, or negative self-talk during the **waning** phase.

When to Use: during the waning moon—especially after emotional challenges, breakups, toxic cycles, or moments of deep self-reflection when you're ready to release what no longer serves you.

Difficulty: ★☆☆ (ideal for beginners)

Time Required: 15–25 minutes, depending on the depth of release and reflection involved

Outcome: empowers you to release harmful patterns, thoughts, or relationships by working with the waning moon's cleansing current—freeing space for healing, peace, and personal clarity.

Method

1. **Identify the Burden**
    - Write down what you need to **release** on paper.
2. **Black or Dark Blue Candle**
    - Light it, stating:

    > "Waning Moon, as you shrink in the sky,
    > so let this burden fade from my life.
    > Drain away all that hinders me,
    > leaving me lighter, freer to be."

3. **Tearing or Burning**
    - Tear the paper into pieces or burn it in a fireproof dish.
    - Watch the remains as a symbol of your **old baggage** dissolving.
4. **Extended Prayer**

- Bow your head:

> "Sacred night, carry these fragments to your sea of renewal.
> May they transform into lessons learned, no longer binding me in sorrow.
> Let me honor the wisdom of release, and greet tomorrow unburdened."

5. Gratitude
- Extinguish the candle:

> "Shadows recede, clarity proceeds—
> I welcome the dawn of a new me."

HELIOS GATE CONSECRATION (RITUAL)

Purpose: Celebrate and harness the **sun's might**—perfect for solstices or any moment you crave **renewed vigor** and outward success.

When to Use: during summer solstice, high noon, or whenever you need a surge of vitality, confidence, or radiant motivation to pursue outward goals.

Difficulty: ★☆☆ (ideal for beginners)

Time Required: 20–30 minutes, depending on your setting, sun exposure, and time spent in reflection

Outcome: infuses your energy, tools, or intentions with solar brilliance—awakening clarity, action, courage, and joy under the empowering eye of the sun.

Steps

1. **Outdoor Setting (If Possible)**
   - At dawn or noon, stand in open sunlight (or near a sunny window).
2. **Gold Candle or Fire**
   - Light a **gold or yellow candle** or, if outside and safe, a small bonfire.
3. **Long Sun Invocation**
   - Face the sun, arms raised:

   > "Helios, Lord of day and life-giving warmth,
   > I stand in your brilliance and open my heart.
   > As your rays touch the land, so may they touch my soul,
   > igniting creativity and banishing despair.
   > Grant me the fire of perseverance,
   > that I may shine in my endeavors.
   > Let each dawn renew my resolve,
   > let each midday clarify my vision,
   > and let each sunset remind me to rest in gratitude."

4. **Solar Anointment**
   - If you have a bit of **sun-charged oil** (like olive oil left in sunlight), dab it on your forehead or solar plexus.
5. **Symbolic Action**

- You may hold a **crystal (citrine or sunstone)** up to the sun, imagining it capturing the solar rays.
- Speak:

> "I seal this crystal with Helios' flame,
> to carry the sun's bold spirit wherever I go."

6. **Reflection**
   - Meditate on how you can embody the sun's qualities: generosity, courage, growth.
7. **Close**
   - Extinguish the candle or let the fire die down, intoning:

> "I bow to the golden radiance,
> thankful for your gifts.
> In my heart, the sun forever beams."

GOLDEN RAY TALISMAN (CHARM)

Function: Carry a **piece of solar might** with you for confidence, vitality, and success.

When to Use: when you seek a boost in confidence, need courage before a challenge, or want to carry sunlight's strength into your daily life.

Difficulty: ★☆☆ (ideal for beginners)

Time Required: 10–20 minutes, depending on sun availability and your intention setting

Outcome: creates a small, wearable charm infused with the solar essence of strength, clarity, and golden confidence—an energetic companion for bold, joyful living.

Making the Charm

1. **Sun Symbol**
   - A small disc of gold-colored metal or a sunny pendant.
2. **Sunlight Infusion**
   - Place the charm in direct sunlight (ideally at noon).
   - Chant:

    > "By the sun's triumphant blaze,
    > I instill this charm with radiant days.
    > Let no gloom overshadow me,
    > for solar light keeps me strong and free."

3. **Optional Additional Prayer**
   - Hold the charm to your chest, eyes closed:

    > "O glorious sun, I honor your luminous heart.
    > As I wear this talisman,
    > let your warmth spark courage within my every breath.
    > May each step I take be graced
    > by your unyielding embrace."

4. **Wear It or Carry It**
   - In times of self-doubt or fatigue, hold the charm and recall the **solar energy** flowing through you.

WEAVING SPELLS – CRAFTING WITH INTENT AND SYMBOL

Spellwork is often described as an art form—a living ritual shaped by color, timing, scent, sacred words, and above all, sincere intention. This chapter deepens your skill in **constructing** spells that unite the mind's focus with the soul's longing.

Keys to Spell Design

1. **Clear Goal:** Define precisely what you hope to achieve.
2. **Align Correspondences:** Match the correct day, color, herb, or planet to intensify your intention.
3. **Use Symbolic Action:** Whether drawing a sigil or anointing with oil, symbolic gestures engage the subconscious mind.
4. **Charge & Release:** At the end, let the energy go, trusting it to manifest in divine timing.

SPHERE OF ILLUMINATED WILL (RITUAL)

Purpose: A flexible **circle-casting** method where the emphasis is on forming a **luminous bubble** of protective and focusing energy.

When to Use: before any spell, meditation, or magical act that requires protection, focus, and intentional space—especially useful when you want a gentler, heart-centered alternative to traditional warding.

Difficulty: ★☆☆ (ideal for beginners)

Time Required: 15–25 minutes, depending on the pace of movement and length of your spellwork within the circle

Outcome: creates a glowing energetic bubble around your space, shielding you from distractions or negativity while enhancing clarity, loving will, and spiritual alignment.

Steps

1. **Select a Candle or Staff**
   - If you have a **wand** or staff, you may use it. Otherwise, hold a **lit candle**.
2. **Walk the Perimeter**
   - Slowly circle the working area clockwise, imagining that each step **leaves a glowing trail**.
3. **Long Incantation**
   - As you walk, say:

       "I forge a sphere of radiant will,
       a boundary of light where none can ill.
       By the warmth of my heart and the clarity of my mind,
       let only truth and love dwell inside."

4. **Mark Each Quarter**
   - In the East corner, raise the staff/candle:

       "By Air's breath, this circle is purified."

   - South:

       "By Fire's spark, this circle is alight."

   - West:

       "By Water's grace, this circle is soothed."

- North:

    "By Earth's strength, this circle stands firm."

5. **Return to Center**
    - Hold the staff/candle high:

        "Spirit, unify these energies.
        This circle is sealed against harm,
        open to wisdom, mercy, and truth."

6. **Use the Space**
    - Perform your main spell or meditation.
7. **Closing**
    - Walk in a **counter-clockwise** direction or simply say a final verse:

        "The circle opens yet remains unbroken,
        I carry its light within my soul."

GLYPH OF FOCUSED MANIFESTATION (SIGIL SPELL)

Goal: Create a **custom symbol** (sigil) that encodes your desire, then empower it with ritual.

When to Use: when you want to plant a specific, focused desire into the subconscious for long-term manifestation—ideal for personal growth, abundance, healing, or transformation.

Difficulty: ★☆☆ (ideal for beginners)

Time Required: 25–35 minutes, depending on how much time you spend crafting the sigil and raising energy

Outcome: condenses your intention into a symbolic glyph, charges it through ritual, and sends it into your deeper mind and the universe to manifest in aligned, intuitive ways.

Steps

1. **Formulating the Intention**
   o Write a concise statement: "I receive financial stability," "I radiate self-confidence," etc.
2. **Eliminate Repeated Letters**
   o Combine the remaining letters into a **stylized glyph**.
3. **Longer Charging Ritual**
   1. **Draw the Sigil** on a piece of paper or carve it into a candle.
   2. **Light Incense:**

      "By fragrant smoke, I veil this space,
      letting the deeper mind take its place."

   3. **Hold the Sigil:**

      "From conscious thought, I birth this sign,
      forging the path for energies divine."

   4. **Raise Energy**: Clap, drum, or chant, building **emotional fervor**.
   5. **Focus on the Sigil**: See it glowing with your desire.
4. **Release**

- Burn the paper (safely) if you used it, releasing the sigil to the universe.
- Or hide it away so your conscious mind can "**forget**" it, allowing the subconscious to do its work.

5. **Closure**
   - Extinguish the incense, feeling a **sense of completion**.

EMPYREAL SIGIL OF FORTITUDE (CHARM)

Aim: Create a **charm** for endurance, courage, and perseverance.

When to Use: before entering a challenging period, during physical or emotional trials, or when you need a lasting token of strength, courage, and quiet determination.

Difficulty: ★☆☆ (ideal for beginners)

Time Required: 20–30 minutes, depending on time spent designing, carving, and energizing your symbol

Outcome: creates a portable charm infused with divine resilience—helping you stand firm through difficulty, remain grounded in courage, and carry your inner fire through all adversity.

Steps

1. **Choose a Symbol**

- Could be a **rune** (like Uruz or Thurisaz for strength), or your own design.

2. **Carve or Paint**
   - Inscribe it on a small wooden disc, stone, or metal token.

3. **Consecration Prayer**
   - Hold the item, recite:

> "O powers of heaven's expanse,
> let my spirit stand unbowed.
> Infuse this sigil with resolute grace,
> that I may overcome all trials.
> In hardship, let me find my hidden might;
> in triumph, keep me humble and bright."

4. **Energy Raising**
   - You might swirl the token in candle flame, breathe on it, or place it against your heart while chanting or humming to **charge** it.

5. **Carry or Wear**
   - Keep it in a pocket or around your neck.
   - Touch it when you need a reminder of your **innate strength**.

SCRIPT OF ARCANE EMANATION (SPELL - MANIFESTATION THROUGH WRITING)

Purpose: Channel your intention through **careful, ritualized writing**, imbuing each word with magical force.

When to Use: when you wish to bring clarity and manifestation to your intentions through the sacred act of writing—especially powerful during waxing moons, Mercury hours, or quiet evening rituals.

Difficulty: ★☆☆ (ideal for beginners)

Time Required: 25–40 minutes, depending on the depth of writing, energy raising, and how long you linger in stillness

Outcome: creates a spell-infused piece of writing that holds focused, personal intention—charging it with magical force and releasing it to manifest through aligned thought, word, and will.

Method

1. **Sacred Writing Space**
    - Prepare your altar with a candle, maybe some calming music or incense.
    - Use a special **pen** and **paper** you reserve for magical writing.
2. **Focus on the Goal**
    - Calm your mind; dwell on the **essence** of what you want.
3. **Write the Statement**
    - In the present tense, e.g., "I am whole and healed," "My business thrives ethically," "I attract healthy love."
    - Write slowly, each word with **deliberation**.
4. **Amplify**
    - Draw small symbols or doodles around the statement if it feels right.
    - Speak an invocation:

> "By the pen's tip and my soul's desire,
> let these words glow with manifesting fire.
> May each letter hold creative power,
> blossoming in the right time, right hour."

5. **Energize**
   - Pass the paper through incense smoke or hold it to your heart.
   - If you have a **crystal** on the altar, place it atop the text to magnify the energy.
6. **Seal or Send**
   - Fold the paper, keep it under a candle or under your pillow for seven nights, or burn it to release.
7. **Trust**
   - End with a short closing:

> "Written in sincerity, sealed with hope;
> Universe, receive my prayer, in light we cope."

By weaving these **expanded incantations** and **meticulous steps**, you transform spellcasting into a **holistic ritual**— melding your mind, heart, and spirit in a single wave of creativity that the universe can't help but notice.

HEALING LIGHT – SPELLS FOR WELLNESS & RENEWAL

Healing stands at the core of White Magic's compassionate mission. Whether you address physical ailments, emotional wounds, or spiritual fatigue, these spells channel **gentle yet potent** energies. Remember: these practices complement, but do not replace, professional medical care.

The Heart of Healing Magic

Healing magic is fundamentally about **restoring balance**. It aligns your body, mind, and spirit with the harmonious currents of nature. Approached with empathy and humility, it can ease suffering and quicken recovery.

LUMINAL BALM CANDLE (SPELL)

Purpose: Ignite a candle that **radiates** nurturing energy to a specific person (yourself or another) who needs gentle support.

When to Use: when someone—yourself or another—is in need of emotional healing, quiet strength, or gentle spiritual comfort. Perfect for times of grief, anxiety, burnout, or quiet transformation.

Difficulty: ★☆☆ (ideal for beginners)

Time Required: 20–30 minutes, or in daily sessions of 10–15 minutes as needed

Outcome: channels calm, loving energy toward the chosen person, creating a radiant bridge of compassion, hope, and subtle healing that lingers long after the flame is extinguished.

Steps

1. **Select a Calming Candle**
   - Light blue, pink, or lavender are soothing hues.
2. **Name the Recipient**
   - If healing for someone else, have their picture or name on paper.
3. **Lengthy Invocation**
   - Light the candle:

   > "Balm of tender flame, I invoke your glow,
   > cradle this soul in warm embrace.
   > Let your flickering light chase away despair,
   > weaving threads of hope in body, heart, and mind.
   > Great Spirit of Healing, guide this flame's gentle rays
   > to comfort and renew [Name] in every way."

4. **Visual Link**
   - Gaze into the flame, picturing the person bathed in a **soft aura**.
   - If you have a photo, hold it near the candle, or place it beside.
5. **Blessing**
   - Extend your hands toward the flame, reciting:

   > "Like a dawn spreading across the night,
   > I ask for renewed strength and bright respite.
   > By highest love, by harm to none,
   > let the healing be wholly done."

6. **Let the Candle Burn**

o Allow it to burn for a set time each day or in one session, always supervised.
o Each time, reaffirm your hope and compassion.

7. **Completion**
   o When you're done, snuff the candle gently, whispering thanks:

"Light of solace, I yield to your grace."

WATERS OF REJUVENATION RITE (RITUAL)

Aim: A **ritual bath** merging physical relaxation with spiritual cleansing, particularly useful for stress, anxiety, or emotional fatigue.

When to Use: during times of emotional heaviness, burnout, high stress, or when you need a deeply nurturing reset for your body, mind, and spirit.

Difficulty: ★☆☆ (ideal for beginners)

Time Required: 30–45 minutes, including setup, soaking, and gentle aftercare

Outcome: blends spiritual and physical healing into one sacred bath, washing away emotional toxins, mental clutter, and tension—leaving you soothed, whole, and luminous.

Steps

1. **Prepare the Bath**
   o Fill the tub with comfortably warm water.

- Add **Epsom salts, chamomile** or **rose petals**, and (optionally) a few drops of essential oil (lavender, rose, or eucalyptus).

2. **Ambiance**
   - Dim the lights, light **soothing candles** around the bathroom, or place crystals (amethyst) nearby.
3. **Extended Prayer**
   - Before stepping in, hold your hands over the water:

     "O healing waters, cradle me in your gentle tide.
     Absorb my pains, my tensions, my fears, and wash them into Earth's vast womb.
     Let every pore open to release the toxins of worry,
     and let every breath fill me with luminous calm."

4. **Immersion**
   - Slowly lower yourself, feeling each muscle relax.
   - If desired, listen to soft music or remain in silence.
5. **Self-Blessing**
   - Cup water in your palms, pour it over your shoulders:

     "I receive this liquid grace,
     cleansing my body, mind, and spirit.
     I am safe, I am loved, I am whole."

6. **Release**
   - Soak until you feel a shift—a sense of **lightness** or **inner quiet**.
   - Let the water drain. Mentally visualize all negativity swirling away.

7. Aftercare
- Pat yourself dry gently, wrap in a warm robe. Sip some herbal tea to complete the **internal** healing vibe.

VITALITY SACHET OF THE GREEN GRACES (CHARM)

Purpose: Carry or tuck near your pillow a sachet filled with **health-boosting** or **calming** herbs, promoting ongoing well-being.

When to Use: during times of healing, high stress, recovery, or simply to maintain balanced energy and restful sleep. Ideal for everyday well-being, travel, or convalescence.

Difficulty: ★☆☆ (ideal for beginners)

Time Required: 15–20 minutes, depending on your pace and how deeply you connect with the herbs and energy work

Outcome: creates a charm of natural wellness that radiates gentle strength, relaxation, and protection—offering daily support to body and spirit through the quiet wisdom of plants.

Method

1. Herbal Selection
- **Peppermint** or **spearmint** for invigorating freshness;
- **Chamomile** or **lavender** for relaxation;
- **Rosemary** for overall vitality.

2. **Assemble**
    - In a small cloth pouch, mix the herbs.
    - Add a tiny **clear quartz** or **green aventurine** crystal for amplifying healing vibrations.
3. **Consecration Prayer**
    - Hold the pouch over your heart:

    > "By leaf and flower, by Earth's gentle power,
    > I weave this charm of vital grace.
    > Let it shield from illness, calm restless nights,
    > and fill each breath with restful might."

4. **Tie and Anoint**
    - Tie the pouch with a ribbon.
    - If you have a mild essential oil, dab it on the fabric's exterior.
5. **Placement**
    - Keep it under your pillow for better sleep or carry it in your bag for daily support.

GEM OF RESTORATIVE RADIANCE (SPELL)

Aim: Channel a **crystal's** natural properties to foster healing, be it emotional or physical.

When to Use: during periods of emotional healing, stress, illness, or when you want to maintain a gentle connection to restorative energy in daily life.

Difficulty: ★☆☆ (ideal for beginners)

Time Required: 15–25 minutes, depending on how long you linger in energy infusion and meditation

Outcome: transforms a crystal into a personal healing companion, charged with your intention and energy—ready to calm, comfort, and restore you whenever needed.

Steps

1. **Crystal Choice**
   o **Amethyst** for stress relief, **rose quartz** for emotional healing, **clear quartz** for general well-being.
2. **Cleansing**
   o Rinse under running water or pass it through incense.
   o "Stone of Earth's wisdom, be cleared of old vibrations."
3. **Charge with Intention**
   o Hold the crystal against your heart or third eye:

> "Radiant guardian of Earth's hidden lights,
> I call forth your healing might.
> Let compassion flow, let broken spirits mend.
> In your crystalline depths, store these energies I send."

4. **Infusion**
   o Visualize **soothing white or pink light** streaming from your heart into the crystal.
   o Feel it hum or glow in your mind's eye.
5. **Amulet Creation**

- Wrap it in wire or place it in a small pouch to wear around your neck.

6. **Use**
    - Anytime you feel anxious or unwell, hold the crystal and reaffirm your link to **restorative light**.

Through these extended **healing** spells, you become a channel for the **loving, curative energies** that flow through nature and the divine. As you comfort the wounded heart—whether your own or another's—you embody the very spirit of White Magic: nurturing, kindness, and deep compassion.

CIRCLE OF PROTECTION – WARDING & BANISHING

Now we turn our focus to **warding** (establishing strong boundaries) and **banishing** (removing unwanted energies, entities, or influences). Advanced witches recognize that true protection stems from both **personal empowerment** and **respect** for the spiritual forces around them.

The Philosophy of Warding and Banishing

Warding forms a **long-term protective layer**, similar to a fortress wall that requires periodic inspection and repair. Banishing, on the other hand, is more **surgical**—it's used when negativity is already at hand. In White Magic, the intent remains compassionate: to **repel or neutralize** harm rather than inflict suffering on the source. These acts must be balanced with a clear moral stance: *"I only defend and restore; I do not seek vengeance or force."*

AEGIS TALISMAN ARTIFICE (SPELL)

Purpose: Fashion a **personal amulet** that maintains a **continuous shield** around you—helpful if you frequently encounter draining environments or negativity.

When to Use: when you frequently face draining people, chaotic environments, or need to reinforce your energetic boundaries with a protective, wearable charm.

Difficulty: ★☆☆ (ideal for beginners)

Time Required: 30–45 minutes, depending on how detailed your inscription is and how long you stay in the energy-raising phase

Outcome: creates a long-lasting amulet empowered with personal energy and protective symbols, offering daily resilience, deflection of negativity, and a quiet field of spiritual defense.

Materials

- A piece of **metal, wood, or clay** that can be worn or carried (e.g., a pendant blank, a wood disc, a small bag containing a symbol).
- **Paint pens** or **engraving tool** for inscribing symbols.
- **Herbs** or **stones** if you're making a small pouch.
- A **candle** (white or black) for protection.
- **Incense** with a protective vibe (frankincense, myrrh, or rosemary).

Steps

1. **Cleanse & Ground**
   - Begin by lighting the incense. Pass your materials through the smoke.
   - Place one hand on your heart, one on the item:

     > "I stand grounded in the light,
     > unwavering against any storm.
     > May this charm reflect my resolve."

2. **Decoration/Inscription**
   - Carefully **engrave** or **paint** a protective sigil or phrase onto the surface. Examples:
     - A **pentacle** or **eye** symbol for warding off evil.

- Runes like **Algiz** (for protection) or **Eihwaz** (for endurance).
  - If making a pouch, place inside protective herbs (e.g., basil, rosemary, bay leaf) and a small stone (e.g., obsidian or black tourmaline).

3. **Long Invocation for Empowerment**
   - Light your candle. Hold the charm between your hands:

     "Eternal Guardian of benevolent might,
     hear my call in this sacred rite.
     Infuse this amulet with unbreakable grace,
     a shield that stands through night and day.
     Let malice find no crack within,
     let fear dissolve before it begins.
     I do not strike nor seek to harm,
     only to keep my spirit safe from alarm.
     Bless this token with watchful love,
     that I may walk in peace, below and above."

4. **Candle & Smoke Charging**
   - Pass the amulet through the candle flame's heat (quickly, not to burn it).
   - Circle it three times in the incense smoke. Each circle, repeat:

     "Protected by flame, purified by smoke—
     I rise unafraid and unbroken in hope."

5. **Wear or Carry**
   - Place it around your neck or keep it in a pocket/bag. If it's for your home, hang it near the entrance.
   - Recite a final affirmation:

"Bound in friendship with light and grace,
this amulet stands as my sacred place."

6. **Periodic Renewal**
   o Re-charge monthly or when you sense the talisman
     weakening. Quick recharges can include sprinkling
     salt, passing through incense, or anointing with
     protective oils.

EXILE OF THE CROSSWIND VORTEX (RITUAL)

Purpose: A **strong banishing** to dispel accumulated
negativity, malevolent influences, or heavy psychic energies.
Ideal when you feel under spiritual siege or after a disruptive
event in your environment.

When to Use: when your space feels spiritually heavy,
emotionally polluted, or energetically unsafe—especially after
conflict, psychic attack, nightmares, or major disruption.

Difficulty: ★★☆ (requires focus and movement, but
accessible to most)

Time Required: 35–50 minutes, depending on your pacing
and depth of visualization

Outcome: summons elemental winds from all four directions
to expel negativity and seal your space with powerful clarity
and protective intention, leaving behind a field of peace and
spiritual strength.

Tools & Setup

- **Incense or smudge** that produces ample smoke (sage, cedar, or a protective blend).
- **Bowl of salt**.
- Four small **colored ribbons** or cords (yellow, red, blue, green) to represent the four directions.
- A **bell** or **drum** (optional but helpful for raising and shifting energies).

Method

1. **Establish a Center**
    - Select a central spot in your home or outdoors. Place the salt bowl there.
2. **Summon the Crosswind Vortex**
    - Light the incense. With the bell/drum in hand (if using), move to the **East**:

    > "Winds of the East, guardians of dawn and clarity,
    > sweep in to banish confusion and lurking gloom.
    > I tie this ribbon to call your breath—
    > gather all negativity, spiral it outward from this realm."

    - Tie the **yellow** ribbon on a doorknob or somewhere in the East section of the space.
    - Move to the **South**, tie the **red** ribbon:

    > "Winds of the South, flame-kissed gales,
    > scorch away malice and ill intent.
    > Let your hot gusts carry away darkness—
    > never to return, carried far beyond my gates."

- **West**, tie the **blue** ribbon:

  > "Winds of the West, waters of cleansing,
  > immerse this space in gentle renewal.
  > Wash away all sorrow and residual harm,
  > that peace may once again flow unimpeded."

- **North**, tie the **green** ribbon:

  > "Winds of the North, sturdy and firm,
  > ground this banishment in the bones of the Earth.
  > Let no foul presence remain,
  > let no ill-thought linger in my domain."

3. **Raise Energy**
   - Return to the center. Ring the bell or beat the drum **rhythmically**. Visualize winds swirling from each direction, forming a **powerful vortex** in the center that **pulls out** negativity.

4. **Extend a Long Banishment Prayer**
   - Over the salt bowl:

     > "By four winds turning, by Earth's own might,
     > by salt's pure virtue and day's clear light—
     > I conjure the Crosswind Vortex here:
     > spinning, cleansing, relentless in cheer.
     > Draw out every shadowed haze,
     > let them be scattered in the farthest ways.
     > I stand in serenity, unassailed,
     > for good remains and ill is unveiled."

5. **Salt Sealing**
   - Take a pinch of salt, sprinkle at the center:

> "This salt I cast to seal the rite;
> no ill returns, by grace and right."

- Walk around the perimeter, lightly tossing salt or tapping it into corners.

6. **Completion**
   - Stop the drum/bell. Sense a calm clarity in the space.
   - Optional: **Burn a white candle** for final purification.
   - Let the ribbons remain for at least one day. Or keep them in place for continuous banishing effect.
   - When removing, offer them to the wind or bury them in the Earth, giving thanks.

This ritual's **vortex** imagery harnesses the synergy of the four cardinal directions, *exiling* negativity and establishing a renewed sense of safety.

WARDENS' VESSEL OF DOMESTIC AEGIS (WITCH BOTTLE PROTECTION SPELL)

Goal: A **Witch Bottle** (sometimes called a War Water or Warding Jar) is a folk-based container spell that **intercepts** hostile energies aimed at a household. Traditionally filled with sharp objects, protective herbs, and personal links, it forms a potent guard.

When to Use: when you feel your home is vulnerable to spiritual intrusion, envy, psychic attack, or lingering unrest. Ideal for new homes, after conflict, or as part of seasonal warding.

Difficulty: ★★☆ (requires careful crafting and energetic grounding)

Time Required: 30–45 minutes, depending on preparation, burial, and level of personalization

Outcome: creates a defensive magical vessel that traps and neutralizes hostility, forming a long-lasting protective ward over your home, household, and energy.

Ingredients

- A **glass or ceramic jar** with a lid.
- Sharp bits (rusty nails, pins, thorns, shards of glass—handle with caution).
- Protective herbs (rosemary, rue, black pepper, etc.).
- A pinch of salt.
- (Optional) A bit of your **hair**, **nail clippings**, or cloth with your name (links you to the protective effect).

Steps

1. **Purify the Jar**
   - Pass it over incense or wipe with salt water:

     "Empty vessel, be cleansed of all lingering ties;
     become a fortress, guarded by wise eyes."

2. **Fill with Intention**
   - Add the sharp objects:

> "Nails and shards, stand on watch,
> barbs that catch ill will and hold it in thrall,
> so none may pass beyond these walls."

- o Sprinle the protective herbs:

    > "By leaf and root, chase away harm,
    > let no foul presence breach my calm."

- o Add your personal tag (hair or snippet of your name):

    > "Bound to me, in rightful might,
    > you guard my home both day and night."

- o Finish with salt, swirling it inside the jar.

3. **Sealing & Invocation**
    - o Seal the lid tightly.
    - o Hold the jar, reciting a more **elaborate** vow:

        > "Wardens of my dwelling, gather in this flask;
        > old steel and herb, vigilance I ask.
        > Turn aside malice, reflect it anew,
        > let it wither, powerless to ensue.
        > This bottle stands a sentinel still,
        > for mine is the right to peace and goodwill."

4. **Placement**
    - o In old lore, Witch Bottles were buried near the property line or under thresholds. Modern homes often hide them in closets or attics.
    - o If burying outside is possible:

"Earth, mother of quiet guard,
cradle this vessel, my home to ward."

5. **Periodic Check**
   o Once a year (or if you sense intrusion), retrieve it or
     visually check it. If it feels "overloaded" or cracked,
     create a fresh one and dispose of the old carefully
     (in a natural body of water or bury deeper, with
     gratitude and thanks).

REDOUBT OF IRON AND BRINE (MINIMALIST PROTECTION CHARM)

Purpose: A simple **folk charm** combining iron and salt—two
age-old protectors—to ward off malicious spirits or energies.
Ideal if you prefer something minimalistic yet powerful.

When to Use: when you need a no-frills, powerful ward to
keep negativity at bay—perfect for travelers, thresholds,
vehicles, or personal grounding.

Difficulty: ★☆☆ (ideal for beginners)

Time Required: 10–15 minutes, with optional seasonal
recharging

Outcome: forms a strong, earth-rooted charm using salt and
iron—two ancient protectors—to shield against malevolent
spirits, ill will, and energetic disruption with minimal effort and
enduring potency.

Ingredients

- A small **cloth pouch** or piece of fabric.
- A **small nail or iron filing** (representing iron).
- A tablespoon of **salt**.
- (Optional) A protective herb like **rosemary** or **garlic skin**.

Steps

1. **Bless the Salt**
    - Pour salt into a bowl, say:

        "Ancient salt, from Earth's deep store,
        cleanse and guard forevermore."

2. **Iron Empowerment**
    - Hold the nail or iron piece:

        "Metal of Earth's core, shaped by fire—
        anchor this charm in unyielding power.
        Stand as a blade against harmful design,
        letting naught cross that means me ill."

3. **Assemble**
    - Add the iron and salt (plus herb if using) to the pouch.
    - Tie the pouch closed with a short incantation:

        "Iron and brine, together conjoined,
        forging a bastion none may blind."

4. **Carry or Hang**
    - Keep it near a door, in a car, or on your person (some tuck it in a jacket pocket).
    - Replenish salt yearly if moisture forms clumps.

HEART OF THE WITCH – LOVE, FRIENDSHIP & HARMONY

White Magic thrives on **positive emotions**—the desire to heal, protect, and care for one another. This chapter focuses on **ethically-inclined** rituals for self-love, drawing compatible companionship, strengthening existing bonds, and nurturing communal harmony. The guiding principle is always **respect for free will**, avoiding manipulative or coercive spells.

The Beauty of Ethical Love Magic

Rather than "making" someone love you, White Magic encourages you to **become** more open to love. The spells below transform self-limiting beliefs, enhance receptivity, and **invite** relationships built on genuine resonance. You'll find no compulsion-based spells here—only gentle energies that **foster mutual growth**.

MYSTERIA ROSARUM – LUX CORDIS INCANTATIO (SPELL)

Aim: Foster **deep compassion** for yourself, healing issues like low self-esteem or shame.

When to Use: when struggling with self-worth, healing from emotional wounds, or needing to reconnect with your inner light. Especially powerful during Venus hours, Fridays, or after emotional release.

Difficulty: ★☆☆ (ideal for beginners and deeply personal work)

Time Required: 20–30 minutes, depending on your pace and time spent in reflection

Outcome: nurtures deep self-compassion, rewrites internal narratives of shame or unworthiness, and invites softness, forgiveness, and divine self-love into your daily life.

Materials

- A small **pink candle** (symbol of gentleness and self-love).
- **Rose petals** (fresh or dried).
- A **mirror** if you feel comfortable gazing at your reflection.

Steps

1. **Prepare a Quiet Space**
   - Scatter rose petals in a circle or on your altar.
   - Light the pink candle in the center.
2. **Extended Prayer for Self-Love**
   - Gaze at the candle, reciting:

     > "Divine reflection of beauty untold,
     > I call upon love's infinite fold.
     > My heart, once bruised by words unkind,
     > I cradle with roses, gentle and refined.
     > Let compassion bloom in my thoughts and veins,
     > dissolving harsh doubts, releasing old pains.
     > I stand in grace, a child of the light—
     > worthy of warmth, worthy of delight."

3. **Mirror Gaze (Optional)**
   - If using a mirror, hold it so you see your face by candlelight.
   - Whisper an affirmation: "I see myself with understanding and kindness."

4. **Rose Petal Anointing**
   - Take a handful of petals, pressing them lightly over your heart or wrists:

     "Soft petals, cradle my soul.
     Let love and forgiveness make me whole."

5. **Completion**
   - Extinguish the pink candle or let it burn a short while in safe conditions.
   - Collect the petals in a pouch or press them in a journal as a **reminder of self-love**.

CANDLE OF CONVERGING PATHS (SPELL)

Purpose: Draw in **kindred spirits**, whether platonic soulmates, supportive friends, or potential romantic partners, without infringing on anyone's free will.

When to Use: when you feel ready to welcome kindred souls—whether romantic, platonic, creative, or communal—without infringing on free will or forcing fate. Ideal for moments of openness, emotional clarity, or gentle longing.

Difficulty: ★☆☆ (ideal for beginners and seasoned practitioners alike)

Time Required: 20–30 minutes, or **10 minutes** per session if repeated over several days

Outcome: radiates a welcoming frequency to attract soul-aligned individuals—rooted in mutual respect, resonance, and heartfelt connection.

Materials

- A **white or pink candle** (for universal or gentle love).
- A pinch of **cinnamon** or **clove** (spices for warmth and attraction).
- A small slip of paper for your desire statement.

Steps

1. **Writing the Wish**
   - On paper, describe the qualities you seek in a friendship or relationship. E.g., "kind, understanding, shares my interests, mutual respect."
2. **Dress the Candle**
   - Rub the candle with a bit of oil (olive, rose, or cinnamon-infused) from wick to base, while sprinkling the spice around.
   - Recite:

     "By scented warmth, I now empower,
     a call to hearts that bloom this hour."

3. **Invocation to Converging Paths**
   - Light the candle, reading your note:

     "Spirits of unity, hear my plea;
     I seek dear kin with whom I'm free.
     Let our paths converge in gentle grace,
     each soul unbound, by choice we embrace.

May respect and joy define our bond,
no ill or force, but a closeness fond."

4. **Visualize Connection**
   - Imagine **light rays** emanating from the candle, reaching out into the world, touching receptive, like-minded souls.
5. **Burn the Note (Optional)**
   - If you wish to release the intention, burn the corner of the note in the candle flame (in a safe dish). Or keep the note in a special place until the relationship manifests.
6. **Closure**
   - Extinguish the candle when ready.
   - You may repeat over several days (re-lighting the candle) to build momentum.

CONCORDIA HOUSEHOLD INVOCATION (RITUAL)

Aim: Restore or enhance **peaceful energy** among family, roommates, or loved ones sharing a living space. Ideal after arguments, stress, or simply to reinforce unity.

When to Use: after tension, miscommunication, or emotional heaviness among housemates, family, or close loved ones—or as a regular practice to maintain harmony. Especially powerful around full moons, Sundays, or in the wake of emotional shifts.

Difficulty: ★☆☆ (ideal for beginners or shared spiritual work)

Time Required: 20–30 minutes, depending on the number of participants and how much space is anointed

Outcome: gently resets and harmonizes the energetic tone of a shared living space, promoting calm speech, emotional softness, and a sense of sacred togetherness.

Ingredients

- A **blue or white candle** for tranquility.
- A **bowl of water**.
- **Essential oil** or herb (lavender, chamomile) to promote calm.
- (Optional) A small **bell** to mark transitions.

Steps

1. **Set a Communal Space**
   - Gather everyone (or perform solo if others aren't inclined).
   - Place the bowl of water and candle in the center.
2. **Infuse Water with Lavender**
   - If you have essential oil, add a few drops into the water. Otherwise, sprinkle dried lavender.
   - Stir gently:

     "Water of life, cradle serenity.
     Calm each tongue, soothe each spirit;
     let compassion flow in all we do."

3. **Light the Candle**
   - Speak slowly:

"Candle of peace, burn bright and clear,
dissolving tension, dissolving fear.
In your gentle glow, we find grace,
so unity can dwell in this place."

4. **Joint Invocation (Optional)**
    - If others are present, invite them to speak or hold hands. Offer a longer prayer:

        "By open hearts and honest voice,
        we choose respect, we choose to rejoice.
        May old hurts heal and laughter bloom,
        forging a haven in every room.
        As one we stand, in love we rise—
        let harmony echo under these skies."

5. **Sprinkle or Anoint**
    - Dip your fingers in the water; gently flick droplets around the living area or on doorways.
    - If all agree, each participant can anoint their wrists or foreheads with the water.

6. **Completion**
    - Let the candle burn for a while in a safe spot.
    - Extinguish it softly, thanking the home's spirit or guardians.
    - Optionally ring the bell once to **seal** harmony in place.

THREAD OF AMITY BOND (CHARM - KNOT MAGIC FOR MUTUAL SUPPORT AND FRIENDSHIP)

Purpose: A folk-style **knot magic** to bind friends in mutual support and loyalty (with their consent). Perfect for strengthening existing friendships or reaffirming a **supportive bond**.

When to Use: to celebrate or strengthen a meaningful friendship—especially after milestones, reconciliation, or as a quiet vow of mutual care and understanding.

Difficulty: ★☆☆ (ideal for beginners and shared rituals)

Time Required: 20–30 minutes, depending on whether charms, oil, or storytelling are added

Outcome: creates a tangible, blessed token of mutual loyalty and love—supportive, respectful, and affirming of each person's growth and individuality.

Materials
- A **length of cord** or ribbon in a color representing friendship (yellow, pink, or green are common).
- Small **beads** or charms, if desired.
- (Optional) **Essential oil** (like rose or jasmine) for anointing the cord.

Steps
1. **Discuss Consent**
   - If you're making this for or with a friend, ensure they are on board. White Magic never coerces or manipulates.

2. **Preparation**
    - If including beads, thread them onto the cord. Each bead can symbolize a **shared memory** or **quality** (trust, laughter, patience).
3. **Shared Invocation**
    - Both parties hold the cord. Speak a prayer together or alternate lines:

        > "We stand in friendship, honest and free,
        > linked by respect and empathy.
        > May this cord remind our hearts
        > that though paths diverge, unity never departs.
        > We honor each other's growth and dreams,
        > and hold each other through life's changing streams."

4. **Knot Magic**
    - Tie **three knots** in the cord:
        - First knot: *"By knot of one, our bond is begun."*
        - Second knot: *"By knot of two, our support rings true."*
        - Third knot: *"By knot of three, in friendship we be."*
5. **Anoint (Optional)**
    - Dab a drop of oil on each knot or simply breathe upon them, sealing the energy.
6. **Wear or Keep**
    - Friends can each take half the cord or create two identical cords. Wear it as a bracelet or keep it in a special place.

PROSPERITY & PLENTY – ABUNDANCE MAGIC

Abundance goes beyond money—it encompasses **fulfilling work**, **creative flow**, and **emotional security**. White Magic seeks prosperity that harms none and **enriches** the community. Aligning with universal **flow** can manifest opportunities, financial gain, or general well-being in ethical ways.

The Ethics of Prosperity Magic

Just as love spells avoid coercion, prosperity spells seek to **open doors** without exploiting others or hoarding resources. The practitioner acknowledges **gratitude** and **sharing** as powerful catalysts.

EMERALD FLAME OF ABUNDANCE (WEALTH & OPPORTUNITY CANDLE SPELL)

Purpose: Draw **financial stability** or career opportunities, using a **green candle** to symbolize growth and wealth.

When to Use: when you're seeking financial stability, new career opportunities, or a general influx of supportive, growth-aligned energy. Especially effective during a waxing moon or on a Thursday.

Difficulty: ★☆☆ (ideal for beginners with strong intention)

Time Required: 25–35 minutes for initial ritual; optional ongoing burning over several days

Outcome: attracts material support, career growth, and honest prosperity—while aligning your energy with gratitude, responsibility, and generous reciprocity.

Materials

- **Green candle** (taper or votive).
- A bit of **money-attracting herb** (basil, mint, cinnamon).
- A small dish of **salt**.
- (Optional) A **coin** or **bill** to charge.

Steps

1. **Prepare the Candle**
   - Carve a simple **money symbol** ($, £, ¥, etc.) or your initials.
   - Rub it with a bit of oil from bottom to top (drawing energy in).
2. **Invocation of Abundance**
   - Light incense if desired (patchouli or cinnamon).
   - Speak a longer prayer:

       "By the winds that carry seeds of fortune,
       by the earth that roots each seed in life,
       by the fire that quickens growth,
       and by the waters that sustain,
       I call abundance into my sphere.
       Let honest work be rewarded,
       let opportunities align in rightful grace,
       that I may prosper and uplift those in need."

3. **Charging**
   - Sprinkle the herb around the candle.

- If using a coin/bill, place it under the candle holder.
- Visualize a **lush green aura** enveloping you, attracting supportive people and situations.

4. **Burning**
   - Let the candle burn in a safe manner—perhaps in segments over several days.
   - Each time, reaffirm your gratitude and desire to share the good that comes.

5. **Completion**
   - Once finished, keep the charged coin in your wallet as a **prosperity token**.
   - Or bury leftover wax near your front door as a continuous prosperity ward.

AURIC CANDLE OF HONEY-SPICED PROSPERITY
(CANDLE SPELL FOR SWEET, STEADY ABUNDANCE)

Purpose: Summon a gentle yet potent wave of **financial opportunity** and supportive connections. The mingled aromas of **cinnamon** and **honey** represent the synergy between **warmth** (spice) and **sweetness** (honey), drawing benevolent abundance into your life.

When to Use: when calling in financial flow, career support, or new opportunities rooted in joy, collaboration, and generous give-and-take. Especially effective during waxing moons or on a Thursday (Jupiter's day).

Difficulty: ★☆☆ (ideal for beginners who enjoy sensory magic)

Time Required: 25–35 minutes, with optional continued burning over several days

Outcome: magnetizes prosperity, allies, and golden pathways using the balanced power of spice and sweetness. Encourages grounded, joyful abundance and magnetism through warmth and generosity.

Materials:

- A **green or gold candle**
- A small dish of **cinnamon powder**
- A teaspoon of **honey**
- A **pin** or toothpick for carving symbols
- (Optional) A small **coin** or **golden token** to place under the candle holder

Steps:

1. **Carve & Anoint**
   - Use the pin to inscribe a **prosperity symbol** (runes, currency signs, or your initials) onto the candle.
   - Smear a thin layer of **honey** around the candle from bottom to top.
2. **Roll in Cinnamon**
   - Sprinkle cinnamon on a plate. Gently roll the **honey-coated** candle in the cinnamon.
   - Whisper or softly chant:

        "By honey's sweetness and cinnamon's spice,
        Wealth and goodwill now crystallize.

Flow in harmony through honest deed,
Let generosity guide each seed."

3. **Setting the Candle**
   - If desired, slide a **coin or token** beneath the candle holder to anchor your intention in the material realm.
4. **Kindling the Prosperity Flame**
   - Light the candle, envisioning a **warm golden aura** radiating outward:

   > "Auric flame, alight in grace,
   > Infuse my life with fortune's embrace.
   > Fire of sweetness, draw success near,
   > So blessings bloom throughout the year."

5. **Completion**
   - Let the candle burn (fully or in safe increments).
   - Retain the coin as a **charmed prosperity token** in your purse or wallet once the spell concludes.

GNOME GUARDIAN'S OFFERING (EARTH SPIRIT INVITATION & HOME PROSPERITY SPELL)

Purpose: Invoke the ancient concept of **benevolent earth spirits** (commonly "gnomes" in European lore) that watch over hearth and home, **protecting** resources and encouraging sustained abundance. This rite respectfully invites such a **house-spirit** into your dwelling.

When to Use: when seeking ongoing household protection, financial steadiness, or a deeper spiritual bond with the land and unseen guardians of home and resources. Especially appropriate at seasonal shifts, new moons, or after moving into a new space.

Difficulty: ★☆☆ (gentle and accessible for all levels)

Time Required: 20–25 minutes, with periodic offerings lasting only a few minutes thereafter

Outcome: respectfully invites a gnome-like earth spirit into your home, establishing a benevolent relationship rooted in mutual care, protection of resources, and the quiet encouragement of prosperity.

Materials:

- A **gnome figurine** or a small stone/wood carving that symbolizes an **earth guardian**
- A **green candle** (optional but recommended)
- A small **offering bowl** or plate
- Grains, seeds, or bread crumbs as an **offering**
- A pinch of **salt** or a purifying herb (e.g., basil, rosemary)

Steps:

1. **Consecrate the Figurine**
   - Sprinkle it with salt or gently anoint it with an herb, saying:

     "Cleansed by Earth, free from strife,
     Rise now as a guardian of life."

2. **Light the Green Candle**

- Position the figurine before the candle and recite a long invocation:

   > "O Gnome of the earthen halls,
   > I invite you within these walls.
   > Shield our home with watchful cheer,
   > let bounty flow, let warmth be near.
   > In gratitude I set this feast,
   > that you may guard our fortune at least."

3. **Proffer the Offering**
   - In a small bowl, place **seeds, grains, or bread crumbs** as a token of respect.
   - If possible, do this regularly (weekly or monthly) to maintain the connection.
4. **Placement**
   - Move the figurine to a **quiet nook** in your kitchen, pantry, or near where finances are kept.
5. **Renewal**
   - If you sense a dip in prosperity or feel uneasy, light a fresh green candle, restate the invitation, and replenish the offering.

ARCANE COFFER OF PERPETUAL BLESSINGS (PROSPERITY SPELL BOX FOR ONGOING ABUNDANCE)

Purpose: Create a **dedicated box** or chest that becomes a magical reservoir for **ongoing prosperity** and **steady blessings**. Each item or written intention inside it amplifies your focus on **gratitude** and **financial security**.

When to Use: when you're ready to create a long-term magical container for blessings, wealth, gratitude, and spiritual prosperity. Ideal for new ventures, turning points, or simply to steady and attract continued success.

Difficulty: ★☆☆ (ideal for beginners and deeply intentional work)

Time Required: 30–40 minutes for initial setup; **5–10 minutes monthly** for activation and renewal

Outcome: creates a magical repository that gathers, stores, and amplifies blessings and intentions for ongoing wealth, creativity, and emotional richness. A living altar to what you cherish—and what you seek.

Materials:

- A **small box** or chest (wooden, metal, or decorative)
- A piece of **green or gold fabric** to line the inside
- **Crystals** associated with abundance (citrine, pyrite, aventurine)
- **Coins, symbolic trinkets**, or images representing wealth and success
- **Paper & pen** for writing intentions

Steps:

1. **Prepare the Coffer**
   - Line the box with green/gold cloth. Decorate the exterior with **sigils**, **runes**, or words like "Prosperity" or "Blessings."
2. **Infuse Crystals & Tokens**

- Hold each item (crystals, coins, symbolic images) to your heart, saying:

    > "Arcane talisman, hold the light,
    > Seeds of fortune, shining bright.
    > Carry my dreams in steadfast grace,
    > So bounty may flourish in this place."

3. **Insert Written Intentions**
    - On slips of paper, write clear statements of your financial or creative goals. Fold and place them inside.
4. **Seal with a Short Incantation**
    - Close the box, resting your palms on the lid:

    > "I seal these hopes in cosmic peace,
    > May generosity never cease.
    > As I give, so I receive,
    > Arcane coffer, blessings weave."

5. **Periodic Activation**
    - Once a week or month, open the coffer, hold a token or reread an intention. Sense **positive energy** surging anew.
    - Replace fulfilled goals with new ones; remove or bury old intentions that have run their course.

CORNUCOPIA POUCH OF FORTUNE (PROSPERITY CHARM FOR ONGOING ABUNDANCE)

Function: A small **charm bag** that continually radiates **good fortune** for finances, opportunities, and general blessings.

When to Use: to attract steady luck, financial ease, and generous energy into your daily life—especially during career pursuits, transitions, or when beginning new projects.

Difficulty: ★☆☆ (perfect for beginners or seasoned charm-makers)

Time Required: 15–20 minutes, with optional monthly recharging

Outcome: creates a durable, radiant charm pouch that hums with good fortune, purifies financial intent, and draws resources and generosity to you and those you impact.

Assembly

1. **Herb & Stone Mix**
   - Select a pouch (green, gold, or brown).
   - Herbs: allspice, basil, mint, or bay leaf for prosperity.
   - Crystal: citrine or green aventurine for luck.
   - A pinch of salt for purity.
2. **Consecrate**
   - Pass each item through incense, stating its purpose:

     "Allspice of fortune, kindle success;
     Aventurine, open doors and bless."

3. **Filling & Prayer**
   - Place them into the pouch, reciting:

     "Cornucopia of fortune, gather here,
     brimming with hope and lacking fear.

> Let resources flow, let generosity rise—
> a cycle of wealth, for me and all likewise."

4. **Tie & Carry**
   - Tie it with a ribbon (green or gold).
   - Keep it in your bag, desk drawer, or hang it near your workspace.

RITE OF AUTUMNAL THANKSGIVING (RITUAL)

Purpose: Express **gratitude** for life's blessings and invite future **fruitfulness**—a seasonal ritual especially suited for autumn, yet relevant anytime you wish to celebrate abundance.

When to Use: during the autumn months (especially around the equinox or harvest festivals), or anytime you wish to reflect with gratitude and realign with the natural cycle of receiving and giving.

Difficulty: ★☆☆ (perfect for solo practice or shared seasonal celebration)

Time Required: 20–30 minutes, depending on the depth of reflection and altar preparation

Outcome: affirms appreciation for what has been received, gently opens your heart to future blessings, and strengthens your connection to nature's cycles of fruitfulness and rest.

Steps

1. **Autumn Altar (If Seasonally Appropriate)**
   - Decorate with fall leaves, apples, pumpkins, or grains.
2. **Lighting a Harvest Candle**
   - Use an **orange or brown candle**.
   - Gently speak:

     > "Season of harvest, I honor what has grown;
     > from seed to fruit, the cycle is shown.
     > I give thanks for nourishment, for support received,
     > for the shelter of home and love I've believed."

3. **Gratitude Offering**
   - Place a **small bowl** of offerings—could be rice, cornmeal, or wine—on the altar.
   - Recite a longer thanksgiving prayer:

     > "Giver of blessings, Earth so kind,
     > I pour out gratitude in heart and mind.
     > In times of want, I found a way;
     > in times of plenty, I share today.
     > May the cycle of giving and receiving endure,
     > that none go hungry and all be secure."

4. **Reflection**
   - Think about **personal successes or blessings**. Name them aloud or jot them in a journal.
5. **Completion**
   - Optionally, bury the offering outside or place it at the base of a tree.
   - Extinguish the candle, saying:

"In gratitude and humility, I remain open to further grace."

EMBLEM OF ASCENDANT VOCATION (CAREER ADVANCEMENT & PROJECT SUCCESS SPELL)

Goal: Boost career development or success in a **current project**, harnessing symbolic power for confidence and favorable outcomes.

When to Use: when pursuing a new role, starting a professional project, seeking recognition, or feeling the call to rise to your next level of purpose. Ideal during waxing moons, sunrise hours, or on Wednesdays (for communication) or Thursdays (for expansion).

Difficulty: ★★☆ (requires clarity of intent and follow-through)

Time Required: 30–40 minutes, with ongoing real-world action recommended

Outcome: strengthens personal will, opens channels for recognition and opportunity, and fuses ambition with integrity—creating an energetic beacon that supports your professional ascent.

Method

1. **Formulate a Sigil**
    - Distill your career goal: "I excel in my new position," "I am recognized for my skills," etc.

- Remove repeated letters, arrange into a **unique symbol**.
2. **Written Petition**
   - Write your statement or the drawn sigil on parchment.
3. **Invocation for Ambition**
   - Light a candle (gold or yellow).
   - Say:

> "By the bright star of my aspiration,
> I rise with clarity and determination.
> Let doors open to honest success,
> let mentors and allies see my best.
> This emblem I forge in synergy divine,
> proclaiming my path, distinctly mine."

4. **Activation**
   - Burn the paper with the sigil (safely) or place it under a crystal on your altar.
   - Envision your career path **unfolding** fruitfully.
5. **Follow-Through**
   - Maintain positivity, but also take practical steps—networking, skill-building, applying for opportunities—to ground the magical impetus in real actions.

Prosperity magic in White Magic underscores both **gratitude** and **community-mindedness**. By sharing blessings as they come, you keep the **flow of abundance** in constant motion, ensuring your gain never becomes another's loss but a **ripple** of well-being for many.